_____

THIS BOOK BELONGS TO

_____

PRESENTED BY

_____

DATE

Illustrated
BOOK *of* MORMON
STORIES

Illustrated
BOOK *of* MORMON
STORIES

Retold by Karmel H. Newell
Illustrated by Brian Call

DESERET
BOOK

Salt Lake City, Utah

Visit us at DeseretBook.com

Library of Congress Cataloging-in-Publication Data

Newell, Karmel H., author.
 Illustrated Book of Mormon stories / retold by Karmel Newell; illustrated by Brian Call.
  pages cm
 Includes bibliographical references.
 Summary: An illustrated retelling of the stories from the Book of Mormon.
 ISBN 978-1-60641-156-8 (hardbound : alk. paper)
 [1. Book of Mormon stories.] I. Call, Brian D., illustrator. II. Book of Mormon. III. Title.
 BX8627.A2N49 2011
 289.3'22—dc23   2011019746

Printed in the United States of America
Publishers Printing, Salt Lake City, UT

10   9   8   7   6   5   4   3   2   1

To my children and my children's children
—Karmel H. Newell

To my wonderful wife, Michelle, and my children
—Brian Call

Contents

How to Use This Book

This book is intended to supplement scripture study—not replace it. The spiritual power that comes from reading the word of God cannot come from any other source than the scriptures. However, spiritual insight and power can flow more freely when readers do not feel confused about peoples, places, and events. As readers (especially young readers) familiarize themselves with scripture stories, the doctrines and truths that those stories illustrate become more accessible to even the youngest reader.

These stories are arranged in the same order in which they appear in the Book of Mormon, but each chapter of this book is self-contained, so children do not need to read the book from beginning to end in order to understand it. Each chapter has sidebars that explain important concepts, introduce essential vocabulary, or offer historical background. The sidebars can be read before, during, or after the body of the story.

The uses for this book are as varied as the families who read it. If, for example, a family conducts scripture study in the morning, this book might serve them well as they read their children a bedtime story. If a family gathers for scripture study at night, this book would be a valuable reference throughout the day, perhaps in a central location, so children can supplement their knowledge on their own. Certainly, this book provides the framework for a series of family home evenings (see page 110). Because the events are retold as stories, this book also lends itself well to discussion and to the bearing of testimony.

Lehi and His Family Leave Jerusalem

The Red Sea

The Red Sea is located between Egypt and Saudi Arabia and is about 180 miles south of Jerusalem. It would take Lehi's family between twelve and fourteen days to walk there from Jerusalem.[1] The Red Sea is the body of water that Moses parted so that the Israelites could walk through on dry ground.

About 600 years before Jesus Christ was born, the prophet Lehi lived in Jerusalem. Along with other prophets, he told the people to repent or their great city would be destroyed. Lehi loved the people and prayed for them with all his heart. One day while he was praying, a pillar of fire appeared on a rock before him, and he had a vision from God. He was so filled with the Spirit of the Lord that he began to tremble.

After this experience, Lehi returned to his home and went to bed. Still overcome by the Spirit, Lehi had another vision. The heavens opened to his view, and he saw God sitting upon His throne, surrounded by many angels who were singing and praising God. In the vision, Lehi saw Jesus Christ and twelve apostles. He was handed a book and told to read it. Lehi read about the coming of Jesus Christ, the Savior of the world. He also read that Jerusalem would be destroyed, many of the people would be killed in war, and many would be held captive because of their wickedness.

Lehi warned the people and pleaded with them to repent, but they did not want to hear what he said. They became angry with him and even tried to kill him.

The prophet had a dream in which the Lord commanded him to take his family and leave Jerusalem. Lehi, his wife, Sariah, and their four sons, Laman, Lemuel, Sam, and Nephi, left their home. They also left their land and their gold, silver, and other precious things and traveled in the wilderness near the shore of the Red Sea. They traveled for three days and then pitched their tent in a valley by a river.

Lehi built an altar of stones and offered thanks to God. He named the river after Laman and the valley after Lemuel and encouraged his eldest sons to be righteous and faithful. They complained about having to leave their comfortable life behind, but Nephi and Sam did not complain. Nephi prayed for faith. As he prayed, the Lord visited him and softened his heart. Sam listened to Nephi and believed in his words, but Laman and Lemuel did not believe.

An Altar

Ever since Adam, prophets offered sacrifices on altars, often made of stones, to show their thanks to God and to prepare the people to receive God's ultimate sacrifice, His Son Jesus Christ.

The Brass Plates

Shortly after his family pitched their tents near the Red Sea, Lehi had another important dream. In the dream, the Lord commanded Lehi to send his sons back to Jerusalem to get the brass plates. The brass plates contained the words of the prophets; they were scriptures. They also included Lehi's family history. When Lehi told his sons to get the brass plates, Laman and Lemuel complained about how difficult it would be. But Nephi volunteered, "I will go and do the things which the Lord hath commanded, for I know that the Lord giveth no commandments unto the children of men, save he shall prepare a way for them that they may accomplish the thing which he commandeth them" (1 Nephi 3:7).

Nephi led his older brothers back to Jerusalem. Just outside the city, they cast lots to determine who should go to Laban's house to get the records. The lot fell to Laman. He went to Laban's house and asked for the brass plates. Laban refused to give them to Laman. He even threw Laman out of his house, accused him of robbery, and threatened to kill him.

When Laman told his brothers what had happened, they felt discouraged and wondered if they should return to their father. Nephi persuaded his brothers to try again. This time they stopped at their old home in Jerusalem and gathered the gold, silver, and precious things they had left behind. Again, they approached Laban. The brothers asked Laban if he would give them the plates in exchange for all of their precious things. Laban wanted their valuables, but he wanted the brass plates, too. He forced the brothers to leave, sent his servants after them to slay them, and kept their treasures.

Nephi and his brothers escaped into the wilderness, and Laban's servants lost sight of them. The brothers hid inside the cavity of a rock for awhile. The two oldest brothers, Laman and Lemuel, became very angry with Nephi and Sam. They began hitting the younger brothers with a rod, until an angel of the Lord came and stopped them. The angel rebuked the older brothers, told them to follow their younger brother's example, and commanded them to go to Jerusalem again. The angel told them that this time the Lord would deliver Laban into their hands. Almost as soon as the angel left, Laman and Lemuel started to complain and doubt. They did not believe that a man as powerful as Laban could be delivered into their hands.

Brass Plates

Nephite scriptures included much of the Old Testament in the Bible and other teachings of the prophets. People did not have their own copies of the scriptures in those days, so whole communities and families shared a set of plates that recorded God's dealings with his people.[2]

Casting Lots

In ancient times, sometimes people threw down smooth stones or colorful sticks in order to make a fair decision. Whoever received a certain stone or stick was chosen to do the task.

Nephi Slays Laban

The Sword of Laban

Nephi used the sword of Laban as a pattern to make other swords. His descendants passed it down to King Benjamin and Mosiah; it reminded them of how the Lord delivered them. In modern times, the Three Witnesses, along with Joseph Smith, saw the sword of Laban along with the gold plates.[3]

Nephi's older brothers were convinced that they could not get the brass plates from a man as powerful as Laban. But Nephi refused to quit trying. He recalled how Moses did what seemed impossible when he parted the waters of the Red Sea. He reminded his brothers of the angel's admonition to go back to Jerusalem. The older brothers continued to complain and feel angry, but they followed Nephi and Sam until they came near the city walls. In the dark of night, the brothers hid themselves while Nephi crept into Jerusalem alone.

As Nephi came near Laban's house, he saw a man who had fallen down, completely drunk with wine. Nephi approached the drunken man and realized that it was Laban. While Laban lay in a stupor, Nephi pulled the sword of Laban from its sheath and looked at its precious steel, gold, and fine workmanship. The Spirit directed Nephi to kill Laban and said, "the Lord hath delivered him into thy hands" (v. 12). Nephi had never shed the blood of a man before and did not want to slay Laban. Again, the Spirit commanded: "Slay him . . . Behold the Lord slayeth the wicked to bring forth his righteous purposes. It is better that one man should perish than that a nation should dwindle and perish in unbelief" (vs. 12–13).

After recalling how important the brass plates would be to their family, and after realizing that the Lord had delivered Laban into his hands, Nephi obeyed the voice of the Spirit and killed Laban.

Nephi put on Laban's clothes, armor, and sword and went to the treasury where the plates were stored. In the voice of Laban, Nephi commanded Laban's servant Zoram to go with him into the treasury and get the brass plates. Nephi carried the plates out of Laban's house and ordered Zoram to follow him.

Not until they met Nephi's brothers outside the city walls did Zoram realize that Nephi was not his master Laban. Zoram began to tremble with fear and was ready to run away when Nephi, a man of great physical as well as spiritual strength, grabbed hold of him and told him not to flee. Nephi gave his word, even in an oath, that Zoram did not need to be afraid and that he would be free if he would go with them to the wilderness. Zoram took courage from Nephi's oath and, in return, made an oath that he would stay with them.

Oaths

An oath is a solemn promise before God. The desert people did not break oaths, or promises, even if their lives depended upon them. Nothing stronger, more sacred, or more binding could be shared among those people than the oath Nephi spoke to Zoram, "As the Lord liveth, and as I live!"[4]

Ishmael and His Family

Jerusalem

At the time of Lehi, the walled city of Jerusalem was at least 125 acres, and the population inside that area was at least 25,000 people. Many of the houses were made of stone and wood, and some were quite large.[5]

While Lehi and his family lived in a tent in the wilderness, the Lord spoke to Lehi again. This time He commanded Lehi to send his sons back to Jerusalem to get Ishmael and his family so they would not be alone. Lehi's sons would be able to marry Ishmael's daughters, and together they could have children.

Nephi and his brothers journeyed back to Ishmael's home in Jerusalem. The Lord softened Ishmael's heart, and Lehi's sons gained favor with Ishmael's family. Along with his wife and children, Ishmael agreed to leave his home and follow Lehi's sons into the wilderness.

As they journeyed, Laman and Lemuel and two of the daughters of Ishmael started to complain again. Nephi tried to encourage his brothers by reminding them how they had seen an angel, obtained the brass plates, and been blessed by the Lord. Nephi told them that if they would remain faithful, they would obtain the land of promise.

But Laman and Lemuel wanted to go back to Jerusalem. Nephi told them that if they returned, they would be destroyed along with the rest of the city. This only made them angrier. They became so angry that they grabbed hold of Nephi and bound him with cords. They planned to leave him in the wilderness to be devoured by wild beasts.

Nephi prayed to the Lord for strength enough to burst the bands. After he prayed, the bands were loosed from his hands and feet, and he stood free in front of his brothers. Laman and Lemuel were still angry with Nephi and started toward him when one of Ishmael's daughters, her brother, and their mother stopped Laman and Lemuel. They pleaded for Nephi's life and told Laman and Lemuel to repent. What they said softened the hearts of Nephi's brothers. Laman and Lemuel bowed down before Nephi and begged his forgiveness. Nephi forgave them and urged them to ask the Lord for forgiveness. After they finished praying, Lehi's sons and Ishmael's family finished their journey back to Lehi and Sariah in the wilderness. Upon their safe arrival, they prayed and thanked the Lord by offering sacrifices and burnt offerings.

Sacrifice and Burnt Offerings

Lehi and his family offered sacrifices and burnt offerings according to the Law of Moses. Their offerings demonstrated thankfulness, devotion, and love for the Lord.

Lehi's Dream

The Symbolism in Lehi's Dream

The tree and the fruit represent the love of God.

The iron rod stands for the word of God.

The great and spacious building is the pride of the world.

The mists of darkness are the temptations of the devil.

The filthy river and fountain symbolize the depths of hell.

While Lehi and his family lived in the wilderness, Lehi had a special dream, or vision, of the tree of life. In his dream, Lehi saw a man dressed in a white robe. The man invited Lehi to follow him, and as he did, Lehi entered a dark and dreary wasteland. After many hours of traveling in darkness, Lehi began to pray. Once he prayed, he saw a large field and then a tree "whose fruit was desirable to make one happy" (1 Nephi 8:10).

In his dream, Lehi picked some fruit off the tree and tasted it. The fruit was sweeter than anything he had ever tasted and whiter than anything he had ever seen. He felt so much joy when he ate the fruit that he wanted his family to have some. Lehi saw his wife, Sariah, and two of his sons, Nephi and Sam. He called to them with a loud voice; they heard him, and they came and tasted the delicious fruit. But Laman and Lemuel would not come to Lehi and eat the fruit.

Lehi also saw an iron rod beside a filthy river and fountain. A strait and narrow path followed the iron rod, all the way to the beautiful tree. Many people started to walk the path, but mists of darkness arose, and some of the people wandered and became lost. Others pressed forward along the path and caught hold of the iron rod. They clung to the rod as they passed through the mists of darkness, until they came to the tree.

On the other side of the filthy river and fountain, a great and spacious building stood high in the air, filled with people both old and young, both male and female. They mocked and pointed fingers at the people who were eating the fruit. Some of the people who tasted the fruit became ashamed and fell away into forbidden paths and were lost. But multitudes of people still caught hold of the iron rod, pressed their way forward until they came to the tree, and ate the delicious fruit.

Lehi told his family about his vision, and Nephi desired to see what his father saw. As Nephi pondered it in his heart, he felt and saw the Spirit of the Lord. The Spirit showed Nephi the Savior of the world. He saw the life of Jesus Christ from the time of His birth until His death and even His return to earth. The Spirit also showed Nephi his father's special dream and explained the meaning of all the symbols in the dream.

The Liahona and the Broken Bow

Liahona

The Liahona was passed down along with the sword of Laban and was among the items that the Three Witnesses to the Book of Mormon saw. The prophet Alma taught that the Liahona is a symbol for the "word of Christ, which will point to you a straight course to eternal bliss" (Alma 37:44).

One night while Lehi was sleeping, the Lord spoke to him and told him to take his family farther into the wilderness. When Lehi woke up the next morning, he found an unusual ball or compass outside his tent door. The ball was made of fine brass, and two spindles were within the ball. One spindle pointed the way they should travel. They called the ball the Liahona, or compass (see Alma 37:38).

Following the directions on the Liahona, they left the valley of Lemuel and traveled through the fertile wilderness near the Red Sea. Along the way, they used their bows and arrows to hunt for food. After many days of traveling, they pitched their tents again.

One day while hunting for food, Nephi's bow broke. His brothers became angry with him. The sons of Ishmael and even Nephi's father complained. Not only was Nephi's bow broken, but his brothers' bows were also unuseable. Without their bows, they would not be able to get any food.

Nephi decided to make a new bow out of wood and a new arrow out of a straight stick. Armed with his new bow and arrow as well as a sling and stones, he asked his father where he should go hunting. His father humbled himself, repented of his murmuring, and asked the Lord where Nephi should hunt. The Lord told Lehi to look at the ball and read what was written.

A new writing appeared on the ball which helped them understand the ways of the Lord. Lehi trembled when he read the writing from the Lord—and so did the others who had complained. The pointers only worked according to "the faith and diligence and heed which [they gave] unto them" (verse 28). Following the directions on the Liahona, Nephi went to the top of the mountain and killed wild beasts for them to eat. When he returned to his family with meat for them to eat, his family humbled themselves, thanked the Lord, and rejoiced.

Tents

In ancient times, living in a tent sometimes represented living close to and trusting in the Lord. Modern Bedouin tents may be similar to those used thousands of years ago.[6]

Nephi Builds a Ship

Ore

Ore is any naturally occurring mineral from which metals can be made. There is a copper mine near the Red Sea that may be similar to a place where Nephi would have found metal for tools.[7]

Lehi's family traveled in the wilderness for eight years. During this time, Ishmael passed away, and Lehi's wife, Sariah, gave birth to two more sons, Jacob and Joseph. Eventually, the families came to a beautiful place by the seashore that they called Bountiful because it had so much fruit and wild honey. After living in Bountiful for many days, Nephi heard the voice of the Lord and went up into the mountain to pray.

The Lord told Nephi to build a ship that could carry their families across the waters. He also told Nephi that He would show him what kind of ship to build. Nephi asked the Lord where he could find ore to make tools, and the Lord told him where to look. Nephi started a fire by hitting two rocks together and made a bellows for blowing the fire.

When Nephi's brothers saw him preparing to build the ship, they complained against him and did not believe he could do it. Nephi reminded his brothers that the Lord would show them the way, just as He had led their forefathers, the Israelites, out of Egypt. But Laman and Lemuel refused to believe and would not help. Nephi reminded them of the Lord's power: "If the

Lord . . . has wrought so many miracles among the children of men, how is it that he cannot instruct me, that I should build a ship?" (1 Nephi 17:51).

When Nephi finished speaking, his brothers no longer dared to touch him, let alone throw him into the sea. Nephi was so filled with the Spirit that the Lord told him to stretch forth his hand toward his brothers, and when he did, the Lord shocked Laman and Lemuel and shook them. At last, his brothers fell down before Nephi and worshipped the Lord.

After being shaken by the power of the Lord, Nephi's brothers helped Nephi build the ship. From time to time, the Lord showed Nephi how to work the timbers of the ship. Nephi often went into the mountains to pray and receive direction, and the Lord showed great things to Nephi. The Lord showed him how to build the ship, not in the way that men usually build ships, but after the manner of the Lord.

After they finished building the ship according to the word of the Lord, Nephi's brothers said that it was good. The workmanship was very fine, and Nephi's brothers humbled themselves again before the Lord.

Bellows

Bellows are a kind of pump made from animal skins that could draw air in and push air out to feed a fire.

Sailing to the Promised Land

After the ship had been built, the voice of the Lord came to Lehi and told him to take his family and board the ship. Lehi's family and Ishmael's family loaded fruits, meat, honey, seeds, and all their provisions into the ship, and they set sail for the promised land.

The wind pushed the ship for many days. Nephi's brothers and Ishmael's sons and their wives began to forget the Lord. They started to be disrespectful; they danced and sang and spoke with much rudeness. Nephi became concerned that the Lord would be angry with them for their wickedness. He had a serious talk with them, but they were angry and told Nephi that they would not let their younger brother rule over them.

Laman and Lemuel were so angry that they bound Nephi

The Voice of the Lord

Elder Boyd K. Packer explained: "The scriptures generally use the word voice . . . And even though it is described as a voice, it is a voice that one feels, more than one hears."[8]

The Promised Land

Many scholars believe Lehi and his family landed in Mesoamerica, perhaps along the coast of Guatemala. No matter where the actual location was, Lehi taught that the land of promise was "choice above all other lands" (2 Nephi 1:5) and those who came to it would be "brought by the hand of the Lord" (2 Nephi 1:6).

with strong ropes so that he could not move. They were harsh with him. The Liahona stopped working, and no one knew where to steer the ship. A great storm arose, and the ship was driven back upon the waters for three days. Everyone became scared and wondered if they would drown in the sea.

Laman and Lemuel still refused to untie Nephi; they threatened anyone who wanted to help him. Lehi tried to convince Laman and Lemuel that the judgments of God were upon them and that the storm would not stop until they untied their brother, but they would not listen. Jacob and Joseph became very sad. Nephi's wife cried and prayed, as did Nephi's children, but they could not soften Laman and Lemuel's hearts. Both Lehi and Sariah were so sorrowful that they became sick and almost died.

After four days of terrible storms, Laman and Lemuel wondered if they would be swallowed up in the depths of the sea, and they realized that nothing but the power of God would stop the storm. Finally, they untied Nephi.

Nephi prayed that the winds and the storm would stop. At last, they did. Nephi looked at the Liahona, and it began working again. Following the directions on the Liahona, Nephi guided the ship until they arrived in the promised land many days later.

The Words of Isaiah

Isaiah was a prophet who lived more than one hundred years before Lehi. Isaiah's writings are in the Bible, but Nephi also included a lot of them in the Book of Mormon. Nephi and his family were familiar with the prophecies of Isaiah. They heard them from Lehi, and they read them in the brass plates. Nephi wrote "that I might more fully persuade them to believe in the Lord their Redeemer I did read unto them that which was written by the prophet Isaiah" (1 Nephi 19:23).

Isaiah prophesied of Jesus Christ in all of his writings. Seven hundred years before Jesus was born, Isaiah saw the Savior in a vision. He recorded details of Jesus' birth and looked forward to His coming. Isaiah wrote: "For unto us a child is born, unto us a son is given; and the government shall be upon his shoulder; and his name shall be called, Wonderful, Counselor, The Mighty God, The Everlasting Father, The Prince of Peace" (2 Nephi 19:6). Isaiah wrote about the life of Jesus Christ, His death on the cross, and His resurrection: "Behold, they will crucify him; and

after he is laid in a sepulchre for the space of three days he shall rise from the dead" (2 Nephi 25:13).

Isaiah saw our day in a vision. In writing about the latter days, he used symbols, or things that stand for something else. For example, Isaiah wrote about "the mountain of the Lord's house," which could be a symbol for the temple. Isaiah prophesied: "And it shall come to pass in the last days, when the mountain of the Lord's house shall be established in the top of the mountains, and shall be exalted above the hills, and all nations shall flow unto it" (2 Nephi 12:2).

Isaiah also wrote about the second coming of the Savior. Again, Isaiah used symbols to tell of the peace that would be on the earth when the Savior comes again. Instead of a wolf trying to eat a lamb, they would live together without fighting. In the same way, the people of the earth would be at peace with each other. Isaiah wrote: "The wolf also shall dwell with the lamb, and the leopard shall lie down with the kid [a young goat], and the calf and the young lion and fatling [a young animal] together; and a little child shall lead them" (2 Nephi 21:6).

The Lord himself commanded us to study the words of Isaiah. When He appeared to the Nephites, Jesus said: "And now, behold, I say unto you, that ye ought to search these things. Yea, a commandment I give unto you that ye search these things diligently; for great are the words of Isaiah" (3 Nephi 23:1).

Book of Isaiah

Twenty-two chapters of Isaiah are contained in the Book of Mormon. In fact, the Book of Mormon quotes more than one-third of the book of Isaiah.

When the angel Moroni appeared to Joseph Smith and told him of the coming forth of the Book of Mormon, Moroni quoted the eleventh chapter of Isaiah.

The Nephites Separate from the Lamanites

Destruction of Jerusalem

Jerusalem was destroyed about thirty years after Lehi and his family left. In 2 Kings 24–25, the Bible records how the king of Babylon, Nebuchadnezzar, and his armies took over Jerusalem. They burned the temple and many other homes; they broke down the city walls, and they drove the Jews into captivity.

After settling themselves in the promised land, Lehi gathered his family and blessed them. He told them of a vision he had in which he saw that Jerusalem was destroyed. If they had stayed there, they would have perished. He thanked God for their safe arrival and reminded his family that the promised land had been saved for them and for the righteous purposes of the Lord.

Knowing that he would soon die, Lehi counseled his adult children and his grandchildren. He promised Laman, Lemuel, and Sam that they would be blessed if they followed their younger brother Nephi. He thanked Zoram for being a true friend to Nephi. He assured Jacob that he would be blessed, even though he had suffered because of his older brothers' rudeness. He promised Joseph that he and his future family would also be blessed, as long as they kept the commandments. Lehi prophesied of a seer named Joseph, who would have the same first name as Joseph of Egypt, and who would bring forth the Book of Mormon. Lehi also blessed Ishmael's family. Shortly afterward, Lehi died.

Not many days after Lehi's death, Laman and Lemuel and the sons of Ishmael became angry with Nephi

and rejected Lehi's counsel to follow him. They decided to kill Nephi. The Lord warned Nephi of their evil intentions and told him to take his family and run away into the wilderness. Nephi, Zoram, Sam, Jacob, Joseph, Nephi's sisters, and all of their families believed the warnings and revelations of God and went with Nephi into the wilderness. They called themselves the people of Nephi.

The people of Nephi (the Nephites) kept the commandments and were happy. They worked hard planting seeds and reaping an abundant harvest. They raised animals, and they built buildings. Nephi taught his people how to use wood, iron, copper, brass, steel, gold, and silver. He used the sword of Laban as a model for making many swords, so they could defend themselves if the Lamanites attacked. The Nephites built a temple like the temple of Solomon, except they did not have the same kind of precious materials.

Laman and Lemuel and their people, however, became lazy. The Lamanites hunted for food instead of working the soil. They depended upon mischief and trickery, and they hardened their hearts against the Lord. Just as Lehi forewarned, they did not keep the commandments, so the Lord could not bless them.

Temple of Solomon

The temple of Solomon was built after the model of the tabernacle in ancient Israel, but it was exactly double the size, about the same size as one of our modern-day church buildings. There was an inner court for the priests and an outer court for the people.

Jacob Meets Sherem, an Anti-Christ

Priesthood

The priesthood is the power and authority of God. There are two main priesthoods within the gospel of Jesus Christ. The Aaronic Priesthood has less power and authority than the Melchizedek Priesthood and administers to the outward ordinances. Jacob and other righteous men at that time were ordained to the Melchizedek Priesthood.

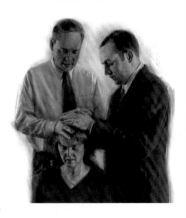

Lehi's fifth son, Jacob, followed after his older brother Nephi and became a leader and prophet to the Nephites. Just before Nephi died, he asked Jacob to write the spiritual history of their people on the small plates. Jacob wrote about Jesus Christ, the Savior of the world. He also warned the people not to be proud. The Nephites were becoming rich, and some started thinking they were better than others. Jacob reminded the people to seek for the kingdom of God before they sought for riches.

Having been called of God and ordained to the priesthood, Jacob spent most of his adult life teaching the Nephites the gospel. Jacob went to the temple often. He prayed, and he heard the voice of the Lord. Angels ministered to him and told him of Jesus Christ. He was the first Book of Mormon prophet to know that the Savior who would come hundreds of years later would be called "Christ." Like Nephi, Jacob also used the words of Isaiah to teach the people about Jesus.

Many of the Nephites stopped keeping the commandments. Some did not listen to Jacob anymore. Many began to believe a wicked man named Sherem, who told them there was no Christ. Sherem was a good speaker who could persuade people to believe as he did.

Sherem wanted to argue with Jacob about his beliefs. But when they met, Jacob was strong in his faith of Jesus Christ. Jacob corrected Sherem and told him that if he believed in the scriptures, then he must believe in Jesus Christ, too, because the scriptures "truly testify of Christ" (Jacob 7:11).

Sherem asked Jacob for a sign to know that what he said was true, but Jacob said he would not ask God for a sign when he knew that Sherem already believed in Christ. Jacob said that if God wanted to smite Sherem He could, and it would be a sign. Just as Jacob spoke these words, the power of God came upon Sherem, and he fell to the ground.

For many days, Sherem lay close to death. Finally, Sherem asked the people to gather around him. He spoke to the multitudes who had gathered and told them clearly that he believed the words of Jacob. He said that he did believe in Jesus Christ, but he had been deceived by the power of the devil. He asked for forgiveness. Then he died. Because these were the last words he spoke before he died, many believed him. The power of God rested upon the people, and many fell to the earth. After that, the Nephites enjoyed peace and felt the love of God for a time.

Small Plates

Thirty years after Nephi left Jerusalem, the Lord commanded him to keep a second record that contained "more sacred things" (1 Nephi 19:5). This spiritual record became what we now know as the books of 1 Nephi, 2 Nephi, Jacob, Enos, Jarom, and Omni.

The Story of the Olive Tree

Pruning

Pruning is to cut branches away from a tree to help it grow better.

Dunging

Dunging is to fertilize or give vital nutrients to a tree.

Grafting

Grafting is to take a living shoot from one tree and join it to the stem and root of another tree so they grow together.

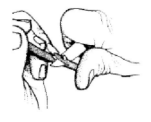

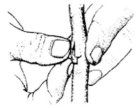

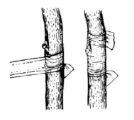

Zenos, a prophet whose teachings are on the brass plates, wrote an allegory, or a story with more than one level of meaning. Jacob retold the story on the small plates. It tells of a master and his servant who worked to grow healthy olive trees. On a deeper level, the story teaches how the Lord and His prophets work to help God's children grow and become all they can be. By using symbols and allegories, Zenos and Jacob were able to share many important prophecies about God's dealings with His children.

The allegory tells of four visits by the master, or the Lord, to His vineyard. The first visit takes place long after the first tame olive tree was planted. That tree had grown old and parts of it were beginning to decay. In other words, the house of Israel, or the Lord's children who had the gospel, were beginning to fall away from the faith and go into apostasy. The Lord tried to stop the decay, or apostasy, by pruning, digging, and dunging the tree. Part of the tree responded to the treatment, but another part did not. In other words, some of the people repented and became spiritually strong, but some began to fall away. The Lord grafted wild branches (His children without the gospel) into the tame olive tree to keep the roots alive. He also took some branches of the tame tree and grafted them into wild trees in faraway parts of His vineyard—some in good soil and some in bad soil. This represents the scattering of God's children, or the scattering of Israel to different parts of the world.

After a long time, the Lord visited the vineyard again. The wild branches had helped nurture the roots of the tame olive tree, and it was producing good fruit. All of the natural branches that were planted in other parts of the vineyard were also producing good fruit. In other words, the people were living righteous lives. The last tree that He visited,

however, was producing both good and bad fruit. Instead of destroying the bad part, the servant asked the Lord to try one more time to save the tree.

Another long period of time went by, and the Lord returned to the vineyard for the third time. The tame tree was bearing only bad fruit. The other natural branches grafted into wild trees also produced only bad fruit, and the bad part of the last tree had taken over the good part of the tree. It didn't matter if the trees were planted in good or bad soil, they were almost all producing bad fruit. In other words, most of God's children who had been given the gospel had fallen away from the faith and gone into apostasy. The Lord wept at what He found. He pruned and grafted and made one last effort to save the trees by grafting the tame branches back into the tame tree.

Many years went by, and the Lord returned to the vineyard for the last time. He called more servants to help gather the fruit. He found some of the roots of the trees were strong, so He pruned the trees. The dying branches were cast into the fire. The servants went throughout the vineyard and gathered the good fruit (or the faithful people) and cast away the wild fruit (or those who rejected the gospel). The trees became good for a long time, but some of the fruit became bitter or wicked. For the last time, they gathered the good fruit. Or, to finish the allegory, the Lord welcomed the righteous people into His kingdom.

Olive Trees

Olive trees are different from most other trees because they do not produce good fruit on their own. Only after a gardener cuts back a wild olive bush and grafts a stem from a tame tree into it does it begin to produce good fruit. It takes about seven years. Tame trees do not become fully productive, though, until about fifteen years after the grafting.[9]

Enos Prays for Forgiveness

Idolatry

Idolatry is when people worship anyone or anything besides God. Sometimes the people in the Book of Mormon sinned by worshipping idols or man-made things. They bowed down to statues made from wood, stone, or metal. Other times, they worshipped their riches, and sometimes they even worshipped a wrong way of life like laziness, jealousy, fighting, or stealing.

Jacob taught his son Enos how to read and write while in his youth. Later in life, when Jacob asked Enos to write the things of God on the small plates, Enos was prepared to keep the record. Near the end of Enos's life, he wrote a short spiritual history.

Enos told of a memorable hunting trip when his father's teachings of eternal life and the joy of the saints "sunk deep into [his] heart" (verse 3). More than anything, he wanted to feel close to God and to know the truth; he felt as though his "soul hungered" (verse 4). He knelt down and prayed all day and into the night. He said he "did still raise [his] voice high that it reached the heavens" (verse 4) until he heard a voice in his mind that said, "Enos, thy sins are forgiven thee" (verse 5).

Enos knew that God could not lie, so when he heard that his sins were forgiven, his guilt was swept away. He was so grateful, but he wondered how it was possible that sins could be forgiven. Again, the voice of the

Lord came into his mind and answered his question. His sins were forgiven "because of [his] faith in Christ" (verse 8).

Enos felt so much joy over being forgiven and feeling God's love that he wanted others to feel the same. First, he prayed for the Nephites, some of whom were no longer keeping the commandments. After pondering and praying for them, Enos again heard the voice of the Lord in his mind, assuring him that the Lord would bless the Nephites if they kept the commandments. Next, Enos prayed for the Lamanites. At that time, they were trying to destroy the Nephites and their records. They were a "bloodthirsty people, full of idolatry and filthiness . . . wandering about in the wilderness with a short skin girdle about their loins and their heads shaven; and their skill was in the bow, and in the cimeter, and the ax" (verse 20). Enos worried about what would happen if the Lamanites succeeded and the Nephites fell into wrongdoing and were destroyed.

Over the course of time, Enos became so righteous that the Lord promised him that whatever he asked in faith, he would receive. Enos cried unto God to protect the Nephite records. He knew that if the Nephites and the Lamanites fell away from the faith, the records would help them come back to righteousness. The Lord covenanted with Enos that He would preserve the records and bring them to the Lamanites in His own due time. At last, Enos felt that his soul could rest.

Just before he died, Enos wrote of his faith in Jesus Christ. He knew that he would stand before Him and again see His face with pleasure. Enos knew that the Lord would say to him, "Come unto me, ye blessed, there is a place prepared for you in the mansions of my Father" (verse 27).

Covenant

A covenant is a two-way promise. In the scriptures, a covenant is usually a promise between God and his children, and God sets the terms for the agreement. For example, people promise to keep the commandments, and God promises to bless them.

King Benjamin

With his own sword, King Benjamin led his people in defending themselves against the Lamanites. He also led his people in the fight for truth, helping them not to believe false teachers, false prophets, and false Christs. "By laboring with all the might of his body and the faculty of his whole soul" (Words of Mormon 1:18), King Benjamin established peace in the land of Zarahemla.

Near the end of his good life, King Benjamin gathered his three sons together and asked his eldest son, Mosiah, if he would make an announcement throughout the land. King Benjamin wanted all of the people to gather by the temple so he could speak with them one last time. He built a tower so as many people as possible could hear him speak.

More people than they could count came to the temple. The people pitched their tents with their doors toward the temple and sat in their tents to listen to the king. He had his words written down and passed among the people for those who could not hear him.

King Benjamin taught his people about humility. Even though he was their king, he did not think of himself as better than they. He reminded the people how he had worked alongside them through the years. With his own hands, he had provided for himself, instead of taxing them or forcing them to pay for his living. Just like them, King Benjamin owed all that he had to God. He taught them that even if they served God with their whole souls for their entire lives, they would still not be able to repay Him for all the good He had done for them.

King Benjamin also taught the people about service, or helping each other. Just as he had "spent [his] days in [their] service" (Mosiah 2:16), he wanted them to care for each other. He explained that "when ye are in the service of your fellow beings ye are only in the service of your God" (Mosiah 2:17).

King Benjamin knew about Jesus Christ and told the people to look forward to His coming, even though it would be more than one hundred years before Christ would be born. An angel had taught King Benjamin about Jesus Christ. The king prophesied that Jesus would heal the sick, raise the dead, and perform many miracles. He told them that the Savior's mother would be named Mary. He knew that Jesus would be hanged on the cross and "rise the third day from the dead" (Mosiah 3:10). He explained how the Lord would save them from their sins and overcome death.

When King Benjamin finished speaking, everyone fell down and prayed for forgiveness. All the people spoke with "one voice" and agreed to take the name of Christ upon themselves. They made a covenant, or special promise, to believe in Christ and keep His commandments. King Benjamin had their names written in a book and called them the "children of Christ" (Mosiah 5:7). Finally, he blessed his son, Mosiah, to be the new king. Three years later, King Benjamin died.

Zarahemla

Zarahemla was the name of an area in the promised land; it was named after King Zarahemla. King Zarahemla descended from Mulek who was the son of Zedekiah, the wicked king of Jerusalem at the time it was destroyed. Mulek and his people escaped. "The Lord did bring Mulek into the land north [Zarahemla], and Lehi into the land south" (Helaman 6:10). King Benjamin's father, Mosiah, and his people discovered King Zarahemla and his people when Mosiah was warned by the Lord to leave the land of Nephi (Omni 1:12–14). The people of Zarahemla rejoiced because Mosiah brought the brass plates. They learned the Nephite language, repented, and joined with the Nephites. The people of Zarahemla became known as the Mulekites.

Zeniff, the Nephite

Overzealous

Overzealous means too enthusiastic or too devoted, fanatical, or passionate.

During the reign of King Benjamin, a man named Zeniff left the land of Zarahemla to search for the land of Nephi (see Omni 1:27–30). He found it occupied by Lamanites. Zeniff went among the Lamanites, first as a spy for the Nephite army to see if the Lamanites were ready for battle, but when he saw "that which was good among them" (Mosiah 9:1), he no longer wanted to fight them. Zeniff tried to persuade his military commander to make a treaty with the Lamanites. Instead, the commander tried to slay Zeniff and anyone else who did not want to attack the Lamanites. The Nephites fought among themselves until all but fifty of their own army was destroyed. Zeniff and the other survivors returned to Zarahemla with the sad news that many of their men had died.

Zeniff was overzealous. He could not stop thinking about the land of their fathers where the Lamanites lived. He really wanted to go back and live there. He enlisted others to go with him into the wilderness. Zeniff and his men were slow to remember the Lord during their journey to the Lamanite land. They had a lot of problems. They could not find food, and they suffered from other "sore afflictions" (Mosiah 9:3).

After wandering in the wilderness for many days, Zeniff and his men pitched their tents near the Lamanite land. Zeniff and four other men went to meet the Lamanite king, Laman. They asked him if they could possess some of the land in peace. King Laman responded very generously. He ordered his own people to leave the city of Lehi-Nephi and the city of Shilom, and he gave both cities to the Nephites.

But King Laman was cunning and crafty. Once the Nephites had worked hard to build buildings, repair city walls, and grow crops, the king wanted to put

them in bondage. He and the other Lamanites were lazy, and they wanted the Nephites to work for them so they would not have to work. Thirteen years after giving them the land, the Lamanites started attacking the Nephites. The Lamanites tried to slay the Nephites and steal their food and animals.

Zeniff armed his people with bows and arrows, swords, cimeters, clubs, slings, and all manner of weapons to defend themselves against the Lamanites. Zeniff and the other Nephites prayed to the Lord and looked to Him for strength. They were blessed, and in one day and a night, they killed many of the Lamanites and drove them back.

Nine years passed in peace, but when King Laman died, his son stirred up the Lamanites to battle again. Zeniff had prepared his people well, though. His spies warned them of the attack. The Nephites were ready with weapons, and they hid the women and children in the wilderness. They were also keeping the commandments, so they knew they could look to the Lord for strength.

Zeniff led his people to battle against the Lamanites. "The Lamanites knew nothing concerning the Lord, nor the strength of the Lord. . . . They depended on their own strength" (Mosiah 10:11). Strong though they were, the Lamanites could not defeat Zeniff and his Nephite army. Even in his old age, Zeniff was strong because he had learned to rely on the Lord for strength. He had also taught his people to do the same.

All Manner of Weapons

Cimeter (also scimitar)

The cimeter is a type of single-edged, curved sword well-known in the Near East during that time period.[10]

Abinadi and King Noah

When Zeniff died, his son, Noah, became the king of the group of Nephites who left Zarahemla. Unlike his father, King Noah was not a righteous man. He was selfish and prideful. He made the people pay heavy taxes—one-fifth of all they had. With the taxes, King Noah built a big palace of fine wood and decorated it with gold and silver and precious things. He married many wives and spent a lot of his time drinking wine.

The Lamanites began to attack King Noah's people and their flocks, at first in small numbers and then with great force. King Noah sent his armies against the Lamanites, and they were able to drive them back for a time. Because of this small victory, King Noah and his priests boasted in their own strength "saying that their fifty could stand against thousands of the Lamanites" (Mosiah 11:19).

Abinadi, the prophet, came among King Noah's people and told them to repent. He warned them that if

Faggots

Faggots are bundles of sticks, sometimes tied together.

they did not repent, the Lamanites would overpower them and take them into bondage. King Noah became angry when he heard what Abinadi prophesied. He commanded his servants to find Abinadi so he could slay him. But Abinadi went into hiding.

Two years later, Abinadi returned in disguise. Again, Abinadi prophesied that the Nephites would be brought into bondage if they did not repent. He also prophesied how King Noah would die—that he would burn as clothing in a fiery furnace (see Mosiah 12:10).

The people bound Abinadi and carried him before the king. King Noah put Abinadi in prison and commanded his priests to gather in council. King Noah and the priests decided to question Abinadi to try to trick him into saying something that would allow them to accuse him falsely. But Abinadi answered them boldly and withstood all their questions. He reviewed the Ten Commandments with them and told them to repent. The false priests became so angry that they stood to lay their hands on him. Filled with the Spirit of the Lord, Abinadi commanded them not to touch him until he was finished delivering his message. They backed away in fear, "for the Spirit of the Lord was upon him; and his face shone with exceeding luster" (Mosiah 13:5).

Abinadi continued to teach them about God's commandments. He tried to teach King Noah and his priests about Jesus Christ. He explained that Jesus, the Son of God, would be born on the earth, that He would suffer and die for all people, and that He would break the bands of death and make it possible for everyone to live again. Abinadi finished by asking them to repent.

King Noah became even more angry and ordered that Abinadi be killed. One of the king's priests named Alma pleaded for Abinadi's life. The king cast Alma out and put Abinadi back in prison. Three days later, after counseling with the other priests, King Noah ordered Abinadi to be put to death unless he would take back what he had said. Abinadi remained true to his testimony and prophesied that King Noah would one day suffer death by fire. They took Abinadi and bound him, beat him with faggots, and burned him. Abinadi suffered death by fire, offering his life as a testimony of Jesus Christ.

King Noah and His Wicked Priests

King Noah was so selfish that his own people eventually turned on him and killed him by fire, fulfilling Abinadi's prophecy (see Mosiah 19:20). His wicked priests escaped into the wilderness, leaving their wives and children behind. They eventually kidnapped twenty-four Lamanite women whom they made their new wives, causing a war between those who were once their own people and the Lamanites. They joined the Lamanites, and Amulon became their leader.

King Limhi Returns to Zarahemla

Jaredites

The Jaredites were a group of people who came to the New World around the time of the tower of Babel. They were led by Jared and his brother, and they were guided by the Lord to the promised land. Their story is contained in Ether in the Book of Mormon. Their civilization lived and died all before Lehi and his family left Jerusalem. Although many prophets preached to the Jaredites, the people became wicked and brought destruction upon themselves.

King Mosiah sent Ammon and fifteen other strong men from Zarahemla to look for the Nephite colony that had left with Zeniff many years before. Ammon and his men wandered in the wilderness for forty days before discovering the Nephites. Not knowing whether the Nephite people they found would still be friendly to them, Ammon and his men pitched their tents on a hill outside the city, and only Ammon and three other men approached the city.

The Nephite guards thought that Ammon and his men were some of King Noah's priests who had been stealing from them, so they took them captive and put them in prison. Two days later, they were brought before King Limhi (King Noah's son and Zeniff's grandson). When King Limhi realized they were from Zarahemla, he freed them. He was excited to know that Nephites were still living in Zarahemla.

Unlike his wicked father King Noah, King Limhi was a good man. He explained to Ammon that they were in bondage to the Lamanites because they had not kept the commandments.

King Limhi gathered his people to the temple. He spoke to them and told them to listen to Ammon. King Limhi reminded his people that during the reign of King Noah, the people had been wicked and killed the prophet Abinadi. Now, the Lord was slow to hear their cries for help. King Limhi explained that they paid half of all that they had to the Lamanites. Even though they had tried several different times to free themselves by battling against the Lamanites, their numbers were small, and they could not defeat the Lamanites. Many of their men had died in battle, and now they had many widows and fatherless children to support.

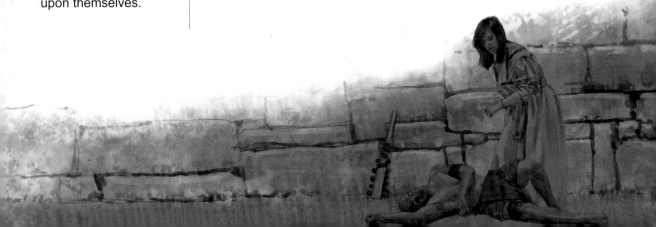

Before Ammon found them, King Limhi had sent a group of men to search for Zarahemla, but they got lost in the wilderness. Instead of finding Zarahemla, they discovered the ruins of the Jaredite civilization and twenty-four ore plates, containing a record of the Jaredite people. But Limhi and his people were frustrated because they could not read it. Ammon told King Limhi that King Mosiah was a seer. He had the gift of interpreting records and would be able to read the record for them. King Limhi was filled with joy!

After listening to Ammon, King Limhi and many of the people entered into a covenant with God to serve Him and keep His commandments. They wanted to be baptized, but no one had authority from God to baptize, so with Ammon's help, they decided to try again to free themselves and return to Zarahemla.

Gideon, the captain of King Limhi's guard, proposed a plan. He suggested that they buy some extra wine for the Lamanites who guarded the back pass. When the guards were drunk and fell asleep, the people could leave through the back wall on the back side of the city. Ammon could then lead them through the wilderness to Zarahemla. King Limhi liked Gideon's plan and prepared the people to leave. The king gave the Lamanite guards a large amount of wine, and the guards fell into a drunken sleep. While they slept, Limhi and his people escaped. The Lamanites tried to follow their tracks, but after two days in the wilderness, they gave up. At last, the people of King Limhi were free! Ammon led them back to the land of Zarahemla where King Mosiah received them and their records with great joy.

Seer

"A seer is a revelator and a prophet also; and a gift which is greater can no man have" (Mosiah 8:16). King Mosiah was a seer who could read the Jaredite record.

Alma by the Waters of Mormon

Mormon

The Prophet Joseph Smith taught that the word *Mormon* actually means "more good."[11] The waters of Mormon may have looked like these waters in Guatemala.

The Baptism of Helam

Alma was not baptizing himself when he baptized Helam. He had already been baptized and ordained to the priesthood. Joseph Fielding Smith taught that Alma's immersing himself in the water with Helam was a sign of Alma's humility and full repentance.[12]

Alma, a young priest in wicked King Noah's court, listened intently while Abinadi preached and prophesied. Unlike the other priests who ridiculed the prophet, Alma believed. Alma knew Abinadi spoke the truth; he had seen the wickedness of King Noah and the other men who called themselves priests. So when King Noah ordered the priests to take Abinadi and put him to death, Alma pleaded for Abinadi's life. King Noah became so angry with Alma for defending Abinadi that he cast Alma out and sent servants to slay him.

Alma ran from the servants and hid. He stayed in hiding for many days, and while he hid, he wrote down all the words that Abinadi had spoken. Alma repented of his sins and taught as many people as would hear his words. He taught the people in private, so the king would not try to kill him again.

The people who believed Alma and wanted to learn more about the gospel gathered in a place called Mormon. Alma stayed in Mormon, by a fountain of pure water, and hid himself in a

thicket of small trees during the daytime. After many days, more than two hundred people had gathered at the place of Mormon to hear Alma preach.

He taught them about faith, repentance, and baptism. Alma explained that baptism was a covenant with God, and that it was a promise to serve Him and keep His commandments so God could bless them more abundantly with His Spirit. Alma also taught that baptism into the Lord's church meant helping each other and standing as a witness of God at all times and in all places. The people were so happy when they learned these important truths that they clapped their hands for joy and asked to be baptized.

Alma took Helam into the water to be baptized first. Alma repeated the baptismal covenant and then both Alma and Helam went down into the water. When they came out of the water, they were filled with the Spirit. Alma baptized many more people that day, but he did not go down into the water with them, as he had when he baptized Helam. All who were baptized became members of the Church.

Having authority from God, Alma ordained priests, one priest to every fifty people. The priests were to teach the people what Alma had taught and what had been spoken by the prophets: the commandments, caring for the poor and needy, and caring for each other. Alma also explained that the priests were to work and pay for themselves; the people should not pay the priests to teach and lead.

So many people joined the Church and gathered by the waters of Mormon that King Noah became fearful Alma was stirring up the people to rebel against him. The wicked king sent his army to destroy them, but Alma warned the people before the army arrived. The people of God quickly took their tents and families and escaped into the wilderness.

Alma and His People Escape

When Alma and his followers were camped at the waters of Mormon, the Lord warned them that the armies of King Noah were coming. Alma fled with his people for eight days through the wilderness before they found a beautiful place that had pure water to drink. They pitched their tents and soon began to till the ground so they could plant seeds and eat fresh food. They worked hard and built buildings. They called their new home Helam.

The people were so pleased with Alma that they asked him to be their king, but Alma did not think they should have a king. He explained that if it were possible to always have good men be their kings, it would be well for them. Alma reminded them of wicked King Noah and how he brought them into wickedness. Alma urged them to enjoy the freedom they had and to trust no one to be a king over them. He taught them that they should not think one person was better than another.

One day while the Nephites of Helam were working in their fields, they saw a Lamanite army approaching. They were afraid and ran into the city. Alma and his people gathered to make a plan. Alma encouraged them to pray to the Lord for deliverance. His faith quieted their fears, and they decided to deliver themselves into the hands of the Lamanites.

The Lamanites told Alma and his people that they would let them be free, if they would show them the way to the land of Nephi. But the Lamanites did not keep their promise. After Alma had shown them the way that led to the land of Nephi, the Lamanites set guards around the city of Helam and put them in bondage.

The Lamanites were not their only taskmasters, though. During their travels in the wilderness, the Lamanites had found and become friends with some of King Noah's priests who had escaped into the wilderness and married Lamanite daughters. The leader of these priests was named Amulon. Amulon and the other priests were with the Lamanites when they found Alma and his people. Alma knew Amulon because they had been priests in King Noah's court together.

Amulon was still angry with Alma for believing Abinadi and defying King Noah. Amulon used his authority over Alma and his people to persecute them. Amulon even caused that his children should persecute their children. Ultimately, Amulon threatened to kill anyone who continued to pray to God. He even put guards over them to make sure no one prayed.

Alma and his people did not say their prayers out loud anymore, but they prayed with all their hearts. The Lord heard their prayers and promised to ease their burdens. The Lord spoke to Alma and told him to gather their flocks and grain and escape during the night. Miraculously, the Lord caused a deep sleep to fall upon the Lamanites. Not only did the Lord make the Lamanites stay asleep while Alma and his people escaped, He also kept the Lamanites from finding them for twelve more days until they were safe in the land of Zarahemla.

After so many years of not knowing what had happened to this group of Nephites, King Mosiah welcomed them back to Zarahemla with great joy.

Persecution

Persecution is when a person or a group of people harass, mistreat, or bully another person or a group of people.

Three Kings

It had been three generations since Zeniff left Zarahemla in search of his fathers' land. His son, King Noah, lived at the same time as Alma. By the time Alma led his people back to Zarahemla and King Mosiah sent Ammon, Limhi (Noah's son) was the king of that Nephite colony.

Alma the Younger

Sons of Mosiah

Aaron, Ammon, Omner, and Himni were with Alma the Younger when the angel appeared. They also repented of their sins. Their father could have made any of them the next king, but they chose to become great missionaries instead.

Many of the rising generation in Zarahemla did not believe the teachings of Alma and refused to be baptized. These unbelievers began to harass those who continued to believe. They even tricked some of the Church members into sinning. The persecution of Church members became so intense that King Mosiah issued a proclamation to stop it. He taught that all people should be equal and that they should think of others as themselves.

King Mosiah's proclamation helped bring back peace for a time, but Alma's son, Alma the Younger, and Mosiah's sons secretly went about trying to destroy the Church. Alma the Younger used his talent for speaking to convince many people to ignore the teachings of the prophet. He stole away their hearts and led them to reject the word of God. Alma prayed to the Lord to stop the rebellion of his son.

One day, while Alma the Younger and the sons of Mosiah were going about rebelling against God and leading others astray, an angel of the Lord appeared before them. He spoke with a voice of thunder and caused the ground to shake

where they stood. Alma and the sons of Mosiah were so amazed that they fell down. The angel commanded Alma to stand back up. He asked Alma why he was persecuting the Church of God. The angel told him and the others that the Lord had heard the prayers of His people, especially the prayers of Alma's father, and because of them, the Lord sent the angel to convince Alma the Younger of the power and authority of God. The angel reminded them how the Lord had delivered Alma the Elder and his followers from bondage to the Lamanites, and he told them to stop trying to destroy the Church.

When the angel left, Alma the Younger and the sons of Mosiah fell down again. Alma was so astonished that he could not speak, and he felt very weak. Those who were with him carried him to his father. When they told his father what had happened, his father was very happy, for he knew the power of God had affected his son.

Alma the prophet gathered a group of people together so they could witness what the Lord had done for his son. The prophet asked the priests to join in fasting and prayer so the Lord would restore Alma's strength, open his mouth, and allow him to speak again. While they fasted and prayed, Alma the Younger lay still.

After two days and two nights, Alma the Younger stood and spoke to those who had gathered. He said that he had repented of his sins and had been born again. He had changed from being wicked to being righteous. He explained that it was like he had been in the darkest hole and the Lord had reached down and lifted him into His marvelous light. At first, Alma felt so much pain for all the bad things he had done that he wondered if he would die, but the pain began to go away when he remembered Jesus Christ and began to repent.

From that time forward, Alma the Younger and the sons of Mosiah taught the people about Jesus Christ. Even when the unbelievers persecuted them and beat them, Alma the Younger and the sons of Mosiah remained faithful. They tried to repair all the wrongs they had done, and they confessed their sins and brought many people into the Church.

Being Born Again

Being born again means to have a believing heart and demonstrate a willingness to enter into a covenant with God to obey His commandments. Those who are born again experience a mighty change and want to "do good continually" (Mosiah 5:2).[13]

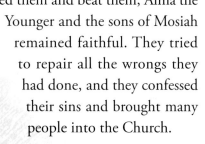

Nehor and Gideon

When King Mosiah died, he left no one to reign in his place. Instead, he established laws and a council of judges to enforce the laws. Alma the Younger became the first chief judge. During the first year of the reign of the judges, the people brought a large, strong man named Nehor to be judged for his crimes.

Nehor had been teaching the people that everyone would be saved and have eternal life, no matter what they did or did not do. Nehor also explained that priests and teachers should not have to work like other people; they should be paid to teach. Nehor introduced priestcraft to the people. Many of the people liked what Nehor taught and began to pay him to teach them. Nehor started to think he was better than others, and he began to wear expensive clothes. He created his own church and tried to sway people to leave the Church of God.

One day while Nehor was preaching, he met a man named Gideon who belonged to the Church of God. Gideon was a righteous leader who, when he was younger, had fought against King Noah and had later helped deliver the people of Limhi out of bondage. When Nehor met Gideon, Gideon used the words of God to resist Nehor's false teachings.

Nehor was angry that Gideon did not agree with his way of thinking.

Priestcraft

Priestcraft is setting up one's own church for selfish purposes, to get gain, or to set one person above others. On the other hand, the priesthood of God is selfless. The priesthood helps all people without payment or personal advantage to any person or group of people.

Reign of the Judges

Between 91 B.C. and A.D. 30, the Nephites had judges who governed them. They had higher judges, lower judges, and a chief judge. After Christ's appearance to the Nephites, the reign of the judges seems to have ended, as it is not mentioned again.[14]

He became so angry that he drew his sword and began to strike Gideon. Because Gideon was an old man, he could not defend himself very well. Nehor killed Gideon with his sword.

The people of the Church took Nehor to Alma to be judged for his crimes. Not only had Nehor introduced priestcraft to the people, he had tried to enforce it with his sword and had actually killed a man. Nehor pleaded boldly with Alma to save his own life, but Alma enforced the law that condemned Nehor to death.

Nehor was taken to the hill Manti to be put to death. Before he died, Nehor told the truth. He admitted that what he had taught the people was not the word of God.

After Nehor's death, other people continued to preach as he had. The people in the Church of God bore with patience the persecution of those outside the Church.

Amlici Wants to Be King

During the fifth year of the reign of the judges, a man named Amlici wanted to be king of the Nephites. He was smart and sly and could persuade people to follow him. He taught priestcraft, just like Nehor did before him. Many people liked what Amlici taught, so they paid him to be their teacher; they wanted him to be their king.

Amlici's teachings worried the people of the Church. They knew that Amlici wanted to destroy the Church of God, and they were concerned that if he became the new king, he would take away their rights.

All the people gathered before the judges to voice their opinions. More people were against Amlici than were for him, so he was not made king of the Nephites. However, Amlici stirred up those who were in his favor to gather separately from the others and away from the judges. In their meeting, they made Amlici the king and called themselves Amlicites.

Amlici commanded his followers to fight the Nephites. The Nephites learned of the Amlicites' intentions and armed themselves with swords, bows and arrows, stones, slings, and weapons of every kind. When the Amlicites attacked, the Nephites were prepared to defend themselves.

Strengthened by the Lord, Alma led the armies of the Nephites in battle against the Amlicites. They fought all

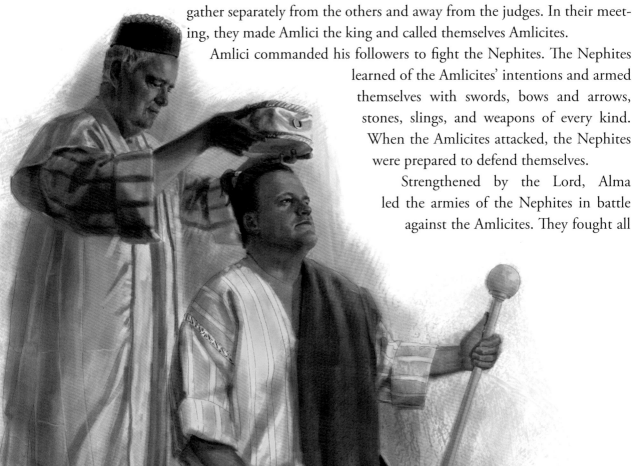

day, and at the end of the day, 6,562 Nephites and 12,532 Amlicites had been killed. They pitched their tents for the night, and the Nephites sent spies to watch the Amlicites. Much to their surprise, the Nephite spies discovered that the Amlicites had joined forces with the Lamanites and were already attacking the Nephites who lived some distance from the city of Zarahemla.

The Nephites quickly left the valley of Gideon and crossed the Sidon River, only to meet up with the Amlicites and Lamanites. On the banks of the river, the Nephites fought the Amlicites with faith and courage, even though they were far outnumbered. The Nephites prayed for help, and the Lord strengthened them.

Alma fought with Amlici face to face. While they fought, Alma prayed mightily that his life might be preserved so that he could help his people. When he finished praying, he fought with great power and was able to slay Amlici with his sword. Alma also fought the king of the Lamanites, but the king ran away and sent his guards to fight Alma. Alma's guards joined him, and together they drove the Lamanite guards back. The Amlicites and Lamanites became fearful and escaped into the wilderness where many died of their wounds and some were eaten by wild beasts. The Amlicites who survived marked themselves with red on their foreheads, just like the Lamanites. They fulfilled a prophecy given to Nephi that those who fought against the righteous would be marked and cursed.

Prophecy

A prophecy is something that will happen in the future that is foretold by a prophet of God.

Valley of Gideon, River Sidon, Zarahemla

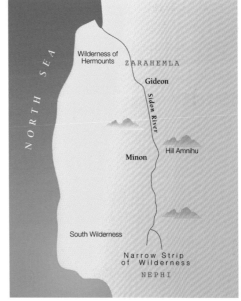

Alma Meets Amulek

Nine years after Alma became chief judge, many members of the Church were becoming prideful. They loved money and all that it could buy and were not willing to share with others. Even those who were not members of the Church noticed their bad examples and did not want to join the Church. Alma became very sad and decided he needed to spend more time preaching the word of God. Alma chose a wise man named Nephihah to take his place as chief judge. Still serving as high priest over the church, Alma gave all his time to bearing testimony and teaching the people the gospel of Jesus Christ.

After preaching in the cities of Zarahemla, Gideon, and Melek—and having a lot of success—Alma traveled for three days to the land of Ammonihah. The people there did not want to hear what he had to say. They reminded him that he had no power over them, since he was no longer the chief judge. They spat on him and threw him out of their city.

Weighed down with sorrow, Alma left Ammonihah. On his way to the city of Aaron, an angel appeared to him. It was the same angel who had visited him in his youth and inspired him to repent. The angel told Alma to lift up his head and rejoice because he had been faithful in keeping the commandments. The angel also told Alma to return to the city of Ammonihah and tell the people to repent or they would be destroyed.

Alma obeyed the angel and returned to Ammonihah by going in another way, south of the city. As he entered the city, he felt very hungry and asked a man for some food. The man introduced himself

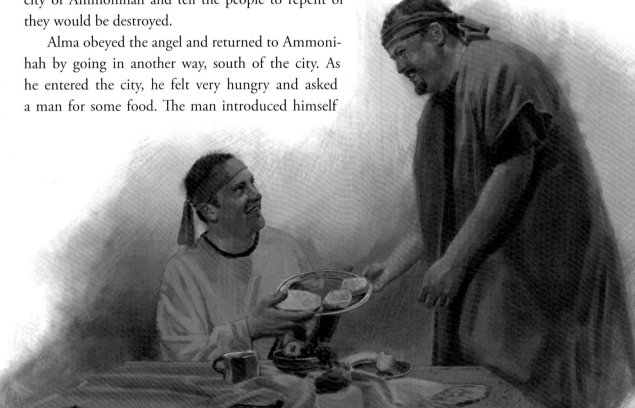

and explained that he was a Nephite. He said that he knew Alma was a prophet of God because he had had a vision in which an angel had commanded him to receive Alma. The man's name was Amulek. He took Alma home with him, fed him, and gave him a place to stay. Alma blessed Amulek and all of his family. He stayed with him for many days before they left together to preach the gospel.

The people knew and respected Amulek. He had a lot of family and friends, and he was very rich. When Amulek spoke, he reminded the people that he was a descendant of Aminadi. With regret, he explained that he had hardened his heart; he had been called by the Spirit many times, but he had not listened. He told them that when he was journeying to visit a family member, an angel stopped him and told him to return to his home and feed a prophet of the Lord. That was how he met Alma.

As they were preaching the word of God together, Alma and Amulek were given power so that no one could put them in a dungeon or kill them. Some people tried to lay their hands on them, but they could not. The wicked people mocked them and refused to repent, but others listened and obeyed.

Aminadi

Aminadi was the man who interpreted the writing on the wall of the temple.

Ammonihah

It was a custom of the people of Nephi to call their lands, cities, and villages after the person who first arrived in the land. No further information is given of Ammonihah than that he was the first man to possess the land.

Zeezrom Loves Money

Zeezrom was a judge of the law who was not honest. Instead of waiting for the people to bring a problem to the judges, Zeezrom and the other judges stirred up the people so they would have more problems and the judges could make more money. The judges were paid a senine of gold every day they sat in council.

When the judges wanted more money, they incited the people against Alma and Amulek. Zeezrom was the lawyer who questioned them. He was expert in the devices of the devil, and he tried to trick Amulek into saying something that he did not mean to say. Amulek told Zeezrom that he would say "nothing which is contrary to the Spirit of the Lord" (Alma 11:22).

Zeezrom offered to pay Amulek six onties of silver if he would deny there was a God. But Amulek boldly explained that he (and all righteous people) would not take such a bribe. Amulek said that Zeezrom knew there was a God, but Zeezrom loved money more than God. Zeezrom kept trying to trap Amulek with his own words, but Amulek was not deceived. He began teaching Zeezrom—and all the people there—about Jesus Christ. By the time Amulek finished, Zeezrom was trembling and the people were astonished.

Seeing that Amulek had silenced Zeezrom, Alma continued to teach them about God's plan of happiness. The crowd of people listened while Alma taught

The Nephite Money System

The Nephites developed their own money system based on different measures of grain, silver, and gold. The six onties that Zeezrom offered to Alma would be worth about forty-two days of pay for a Nephite judge.[15]

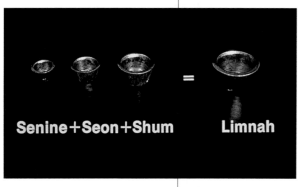

Senine + Seon + Shum = Limnah

Zeezrom. Alma began by telling Zeezrom that not only had he lied to men like Amulek, he had also lied to God. Zeezrom began to tremble even more as he became convinced of his own sins and of God's power. He began to ask Alma sincere questions. Alma taught him about repentance and preparing to meet God by living righteously. A chief ruler, Antionah, also came forward and asked Alma questions about the resurrection.

Most of the people did not like what Alma said. They did not want to hear that they needed to repent, so they took Alma and Amulek and bound them and put them into prison. Meanwhile, Zeezrom thought about what they taught. Zeezrom felt so sorry for what he had done that he became very ill with a fever. After some time, he sent for Alma and Amulek. He told them that he believed in Jesus Christ, and he asked them if they would heal him. After Alma blessed him, Zeezrom leaped to his feet and began to walk. The people were amazed. Alma baptized Zeezrom, and Zeezrom preached the true gospel of Jesus Christ to other people for the rest of his life.

Alma and Amulek in Prison

Order of Nehor

The teachers, judges, and lawyers who were of the order of Nehor were a prideful group of people who were not truly religious. They wore expensive clothes and paid their religious leaders to say what they wanted to hear. They misled the people by teaching them that it did not matter if they sinned because they would all end up in paradise.

When Alma finished teaching in Ammonihah, many people believed what he had taught; they repented and began to search the scriptures. But more of the people were angry. They did not want to hear that they needed to repent, so they bound Alma and Amulek with strong cords and took them before the chief judge. Wicked people bore false witness against Alma and Amulek. They threw those who believed Alma and Amulek out of the city, and they sent men to throw stones at them.

The wicked people gathered the wives and children of those who believed Alma and Amulek, along with anyone else who believed or had been taught to believe in the word of God. The wicked people threw the believers into a big fire. They also threw their scriptures into the fire. They brought Alma and Amulek to watch the righteous people being killed. Amulek could not bear to watch them suffer and die, so he asked Alma if they should use the power of God to save them. But Alma told Amulek that the Spirit would not let him. He explained that the Lord would receive the believers into His glory, and their innocence would testify against the wicked people in the day of judgment.

The wicked people took Alma and Amulek back to the chief judge. He hit them on the face and asked them if they would continue to preach the word of God after what they had seen. Alma and Amulek refused to speak. He hit them again and told his officers to put them in prison. After three days in prison, many lawyers, judges, and teachers after the order of Nehor came to question them, but Alma and Amulek would not answer their questions. The chief judge commanded them to speak, but they said nothing.

The wicked judges, lawyers, and teachers returned to Alma and Amulek in prison. They spat on them, mocked them, and refused to give them food or water. The chief judge continued to beat them. For many days, Alma and Amulek stayed in prison without food or water. The wicked people even stripped Alma and Amulek of their clothes and bound them with strong cords. The chief judge and the other wicked people returned again: hitting, insulting, and provoking Alma and Amulek. One by one, the chief judge and all of the others hit Alma and Amulek and challenged them to use the power of God to save themselves.

Finally, Alma and Amulek stood. The power of God rested upon them. Alma prayed out loud, and Alma and Amulek miraculously broke the strong cords tied around them. When the wicked people saw this, they became afraid and started to run. The wicked people were so afraid that they fell down. The earth shook mightily, and the prison walls broke, crumbled, and fell on the chief judge and all the other wicked people. Everyone who had been in the prison was killed, except Alma and Amulek. People heard the great noise of the prison collapsing, and they came to see what had happened. When they saw Alma and Amulek walk out of the prison unharmed and everyone else dead inside, they ran away in fear.

Alma and Amulek left the city and went to Sidom to minister to those who believed their words but had been forced to leave Ammonihah.

Amulek was especially sad because he had been rejected by his own father, his family, and those who were once his friends. Alma took Amulek to his own home to care for him and strengthen him.

The Sons of King Mosiah

Ammon, Aaron, Omner, and Himni were the sons of King Mosiah. They were with Alma the Younger at the time he saw an angel and repented of his sins. They, too, saw the angel and repented. They stopped trying to destroy the Church of God. Even though they had been wicked, they really changed. They suffered a lot of pain and sorrow as they realized their sins. They went with Alma the Younger all around Zarahemla, admitting that they had been wrong and trying to repair the bad things they had done. They explained their change of heart and shared the teachings of the prophets and the scriptures with anyone who would listen. They became powerful missionaries, bringing peace and joy to many people.

After serving the people of Zarahemla, the sons of Mosiah wanted to preach the gospel to the Lamanites, a wild and bloodthirsty people. They pleaded with their father for many days for him to give them permission to serve the Lamanites. Each son told his father that he would rather be a missionary than become the next king. King Mosiah prayed and asked the Lord if he should let his sons go. The Lord told Mosiah that he should

allow his sons to serve the Lamanites, that many would believe what they taught, and that the Lord would preserve their lives.

The sons of Mosiah journeyed for many days in the wilderness before they reached the Lamanites. They took weapons with them so they could find food for themselves. They fasted and prayed for the Lord to bless them with His Spirit. When they reached the borders of the land of the Lamanites, they separated; each missionary left to teach the gospel in a different region.

The sons of Mosiah were often hungry, thirsty, and tired, yet they continued to preach the word of God. They were even put in prison, but they were miraculously delivered. Many of the Lamanites rejected them, but many also received them. The Lord blessed and watched over them, and they brought many Lamanites, even kings, to a knowledge of the truth. Eventually, the king over all the other kings sent a proclamation to the Lamanites that they should not harm the missionaries or put them in prison. He told his people to give them free access to their homes, temples, and sanctuaries so they could preach the word of God. The sons of Mosiah served as missionaries to the Lamanites for fourteen years.

A Joyful Reunion

On their way home from their mission to the Lamanites, the sons of Mosiah ran into their old friend, Alma the Younger. They were surprised to see each other; it had been a long time since they had been together. Alma was very happy that they were "still his brethren in the Lord; yea, and they had waxed strong in the knowledge of the truth" (Alma 17:2).

Ammon, the Missionary

Flocks

A flock is a group of animals, often sheep or maybe cattle, that live, travel, and feed together. The Book of Mormon records twelve different kinds of animals: cow, dog, goat, wild goat, horse, sheep, ox, ass, swine, elephant, "curelom," and "cumom."[16]

We do not know if the animals looked like our animals today. A horse may have been more like a deer, and an elephant may have been more like a mammoth. Or they may have been just the same. What do you think cureloms and cumoms were like?

Ammon, one of the sons of King Mosiah, could have become the king, but instead he chose to serve a mission to the Lamanites. He fasted and prayed and prepared himself to serve. He blessed his brothers and then left for the land of Ishmael. Ammon took weapons with him so he could provide food for himself while he traveled and taught.

When he entered the land of Ishmael, the Lamanites bound him and brought him before King Lamoni—as they did with any Nephite who crossed their borders. King Lamoni asked Ammon if he wanted to live among them, and Ammon said that he did, maybe even for the rest of his life. King Lamoni was pleased with Ammon and asked him if he wanted to marry one of his daughters. Ammon said that he did not, but that he would be the king's servant.

Along with other servants, Ammon was assigned to watch over the king's flocks. A few days after he had arrived, Ammon was leading the flocks to drinking water when enemies of the king scattered the flocks. The servants began to cry, saying that the king would kill them, as he had the other servants who had lost the king's flocks.

Ammon told the servants to cheer up and search for the flocks. He led the way as they hurried toward the lost animals. Ammon and the other servants herded the flocks and gathered them back to the place of water. The enemies tried to scatter the flocks again. This time, Ammon told the servants to watch the flocks while he contended with the men. At first, he threw stones at the men, and six of them fell. The ones left standing were surprised by Ammon's power and skill. They could not hit him with stones, so they came at him with clubs. Ammon cut off the arms of every man who raised a club to kill him, and he killed their leader. Even

though there were many of them, they eventually ran away from Ammon in fear.

When he had driven them far off, Ammon went back to the flocks and the other servants. The sevants returned to King Lamoni, carrying the arms that Ammon had cut off with his sword. The king spoke with the servants alone and asked them to explain what Ammon had done. They told him how Ammon had defended the king's flocks single-handedly.

King Lamoni was very amazed, and he thought Ammon might be the Great Spirit—the god his fathers had told him would come. The king began to feel guilty, wondering if maybe the Great Spirit visited them because the king had killed the other servants who did not protect his flocks. When King Lamoni wondered where Ammon was, the servants told him that Ammon was doing what the king had asked: feeding the king's horses and preparing the chariots so the king could visit his father.

When Ammon finished taking care of the horses, he came to the king but noticed that the king looked different. Ammon asked what he should do for the king, but the king was so awestruck that he did not answer his question for an hour. The Spirit of the Lord was with Ammon, and he could tell what the king was thinking. The king marveled that Ammon knew his thoughts. Ammon told the king that he was a man, not the Great Spirit, and then Ammon began to teach the king the gospel.

The Great Spirit

The Lamanites taught that God is the Great Spirit, a glorious person, who watched over them and would come among them. This same idea existed among American Indians in more modern times.[17]

King Lamoni's Conversion

After Ammon saved King Lamoni's flocks and cared for his horses, he spoke boldly to the king about the gospel of Jesus Christ. Ammon taught him about God and the teachings of the prophets in the scriptures. He also reviewed the history of their people. Ammon explained the plan of salvation and told the king and his servants to look forward to the coming of Christ. King Lamoni listened and believed.

When Ammon finished, the king prayed out loud that the Lord would forgive him and be merciful to him and to his people. As soon as he prayed, King Lamoni fell down, as if he were dead. The servants carried him to his wife and laid him on his bed. For two days, King Lamoni lay still. His family mourned over him and thought he might have died. The servants told the queen about Ammon and his great power, so she sent for him. She told Ammon that she did not think the king was dead, but that everyone else thought they should put King Lamoni in a sepulchre.

Ammon saw the king on his bed and told the queen that the king was not dead; he was "sleeping in God," and he would rise again the next day. The queen believed Ammon and watched over her husband. Just as Ammon foretold, King Lamoni rose from his bed the next day. The king reached for his wife and told her that as surely as she lived, he had seen Jesus. He was so filled with joy that he collapsed again, and the queen also fell down, being overpowered by the Spirit.

Ammon saw how his prayers for them were being answered, and he knelt down to thank God. Ammon was so filled with joy that he fell down, along with the king and the queen. When the servants saw what had happened, they, too, began to pray. They were so overcome with joy that they also fell down—except for one servant named Abish. She had converted to the Lord many years earlier when her father had a remarkable vision. She knew the power of God was upon them, so she ran from house to house telling the people what had happened.

A crowd of people gathered at the king's house. Some thought evil had come upon them. Some thought Ammon was the Great Spirit. They argued among themselves about what power held the king, the queen, Ammon, and the servants. One man whose brother had been slain by Ammon (while he was defending the king's flocks) drew his sword to kill Ammon, but just as he lifted his sword, the man fell dead. The crowd saw how the man died instantly and became afraid.

While the crowd argued among themselves, Abish became sad and began to cry. She took the queen by the hand, and as she touched her hand, the queen stood and said, "O blessed Jesus." After the queen spoke, she clasped her hands with joy and then took the king by the hand. He stood, scolded the people for arguing, and repeated Ammon's teachings. The servants also stood and explained that their hearts had been changed. They told the people that they had seen and spoken with angels. Many of the people listened and believed; many others would not listen. Those who believed were baptized, and Ammon established a church among them.

Sepulchre

A sepulchre is a burial tomb, a vault, or a grave.

King Lamoni's Father

King Lamoni wanted Ammon to meet his father, the old Lamanite king who ruled over all the land. But Ammon was warned not to go. The voice of the Lord told Ammon that King Lamoni's father would try to kill him. Instead, Ammon was told that he should go to Middoni to free his brother and friends who were in prison. When King Lamoni asked Ammon how he knew they were in prison, Ammon explained that God had told him.

King Lamoni wanted to go with Ammon to Middoni. He told Ammon that the king over Middoni was a friend of his, and he could plead with him to free Ammon's brother and friends. King Lamoni asked his servants to prepare his horses and chariots, and they left for Middoni together.

While King Lamoni and Ammon were traveling, they ran into King Lamoni's father. He was upset with his son and asked why he had not come to his great feast. He also wondered why he was traveling with one of their enemies, a Nephite. King Lamoni tried to tell his father that Ammon was his friend, and he tried to explain why he had not come to the feast, but his father was angry with him and commanded him to kill Ammon.

King Lamoni refused to slay his new friend, Ammon. King Lamoni's father became so angry that he drew his sword to kill his own son, but Ammon stopped him. King Lamoni's father then turned his anger on Ammon and tried to kill him, but Ammon resisted him and wounded the old king's arm. When King Lamoni's father realized that Ammon could kill him, he pleaded for his life. He promised that if Ammon would spare his life, he would give him whatever he asked, even half of his kingdom.

Ammon released the old king and asked him only to free his brother and friends in Middoni and allow Lamoni to keep his kingdom, the land of Ishmael. When the old king saw that Ammon did not want to destroy him, he rejoiced. King Lamoni's father was astonished by Ammon's great love for his son. He allowed Lamoni to keep his kingdom, promising not to rule over him anymore. He also agreed to free Ammon's brother and friends who were in prison and even invited them to come and see him in the land of Nephi.

After Ammon and King Lamoni delivered them from prison, Aaron and his companions were led by the Spirit to the land of Nephi, to King Lamoni's father. They went to the palace and bowed down to the old king and offered to be his servants. But the king told them he did not want them to be servants; he wanted them to teach him. Aaron and his companions taught him about Jesus Christ. The old king listened and believed. He said he would give up everything he owned, even his kingdom, to feel the joy they described.

Aaron and the sons of Mosiah taught King Lamoni's father how to repent and to pray. The old king first knelt and then lay flat on the floor to pray for forgiveness. When he finished praying, he was struck as if he were dead. The queen became worried and sent her servants to get help. Aaron, fearing the people would not understand and would begin to fight, reached his hand to the king and raised him up. The king stood and ministered to the queen and his household, and they were all converted to the Lord.

Land of Nephi

Located south of Zarahemla and bordered by water on the east and west, the land of Nephi was controlled by Nephites until Mosiah left (about 200 B.C.) and then by Lamanites throughout the rest of the Book of Mormon.[18]

The Anti-Nephi-Lehies

After his conversion, King Lamoni's father sent a proclamation throughout all the Lamanite lands telling his people not to lay their hands on Ammon, Aaron, Omner, Himni, or any of the other missionaries. He ordered his people not to put them in prison, hit them, throw stones at them, or push them out of their synagogues. He wanted the missionaries to be able to teach the word of God to all the people without difficulty.

The sons of Mosiah and other missionaries traveled from one Lamanite city to another, teaching the people about Jesus Christ, establishing churches, and setting apart priests and teachers. They taught them from the scriptures and helped them become familiar with Nephite records and prophecies. They had so much success that thousands were brought to believe in the Lord.

After receiving the gospel, King Lamoni's father and other converts decided to call themselves Anti-Nephi-Lehies, so they would no longer be known as Lamanites. Before the old king died, he conferred the kingdom on his son whom he named Anti-Nephi-Lehi. Like his brother Lamoni, Anti-Nephi-Lehi had listened to the missionaries and become a righteous leader. He counseled with Ammon and the sons of Mosiah to know how to defend themselves against the Lamanites, especially the Amalekites and the Amulonites, who were preparing to go to war against them. The Anti-Nephi-Lehies had become so righteous that they refused to use their weapons anymore. Their king agreed that they should not. He was so grateful to have been forgiven of the many sins and murders they had committed in the past that he could not ask them to stain their swords with blood again. So the Anti-Nephi-Lehies buried their weapons deep in the earth, as a testimony to God and to men of their complete repentance. They decided they would rather die than commit serious sins like murder ever again.

When the Lamanites came upon them, the Anti-Nephi-Lehies went out to meet them. They lay on their stomachs with their heads down. They prayed. The Lamanites fell upon them and began to slay them with their swords. The Anti-Nephi-Lehies did not fight back; they praised God even while they were dying. One thousand and five of them were killed before the Lamanites stopped. Many of the Lamanites threw down their weapons and refused to continue killing. Their hearts were touched, and they wanted to repent. In fact, more than a thousand Lamanites joined the people of God that day. Like the Anti-Nephi-Lehies, they wanted peace with God and with each other.

Anti-Nephi-Lehi

"Anti-Nephi Lehi" is the name of Lamoni's brother who became king over all the land. It is also the name for the righteous group of converts who no longer wanted to be known as Lamanites. In ancient Egyptian (from which it was translated), "anti" likely means "one of," not "against" like we think of it today. So Anti-Nephi-Lehi was someone who was "one of" the Nephites.[19]

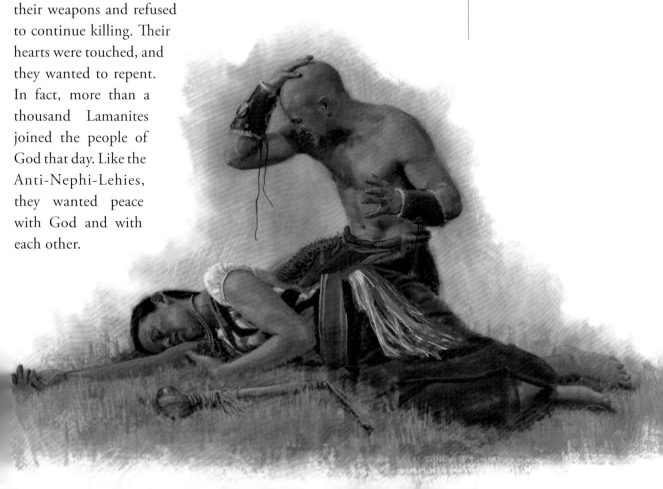

Ammon Asks God

Near the end of Ammon's mission, the wicked Lamanites tried to destroy the Nephites again. After many struggles, the Lamanites decided it was useless, so they returned to their own land. The Amalekites were so angry about losing to the Nephites that they stirred up the Lamanites to fight against the Lamanite converts, the Anti-Nephi-Lehies.

When Ammon saw how the Anti-Nephi-Lehies refused to fight again and would rather die than take up their weapons of war, he gathered all the people of the Lord together. He suggested that they return with him to Zarahemla and seek protection there. King Lamoni feared that the Nephites would not accept his people; he worried they would try to destroy them because of the murders and sins they had committed in the past. The king suggested that he and his people could be slaves to the Nephites until they repaired their many wrongs, but Ammon explained that it was against the law to have slaves in Zarahemla. Ammon told the king he would pray and ask God if it would be safe for the Anti-Nephi-Lehies to go home with him.

After Ammon prayed, the Lord told him to take the Anti-Nephi-Lehies out of the land of Nephi and return to Zarahemla. The Anti-Nephi-Lehies waited in the wilderness on the borders of Zarahemla, while Ammon and his brothers went to talk to the Nephites to see how they would feel about accepting their one-time enemies.

On their way, Ammon and his brothers ran into

Amalekites

The Amalekites were former Nephites who rejected the prophecies about Christ and who lived among the Lamanites. They became more wicked and murderous than the actual Lamanites.

their old friend Alma. He, too, had remained faithful and was a powerful servant of the Lord. They rejoiced to be together again, and even more, to have stayed true to the covenants they made many years earlier when they became converted to the truth. Their hearts were filled with joy, and Alma welcomed them into his home.

The chief judge sent a proclamation throughout the land, asking the Nephites how they felt about allowing the Anti-Nephi-Lehies to live within their borders. In the spirit of forgiveness, the Nephites responded by saying they would give the Lamanite converts the land of Jershon, and they would even use their own armies to defend it. The Nephites promised to protect the Anti-Nephi-Lehies from their enemies and only asked that they help care for the soldiers.

Ammon told King Lamoni the good news, and the Anti-Nephi-Lehies rejoiced to be welcomed by the Nephites. So fourteen years after he left to serve a mission to the Lamanites, Ammon returned home with thousands of converts. From that time forward, the Nephites called the Anti-Nephi-Lehies the people of Ammon.

Proclamation

A proclamation is an official, formal public announcement.

Alma Silences Korihor

After the great war between the Nephites and the Lamanites in the fifteenth year of the reign of judges, there was a brief period of peace throughout the land. Then a man named Korihor came to Zarahemla and started preaching against the prophecies of Christ. He told the Nephites that their belief in Christ was a foolish hope because no one could know what would happen in the future. He convinced many of them that they were crazy to hold onto traditions that they could not prove were true. Instead of looking to God for strength, he taught them to depend upon their own power and skill. Korihor led many of the Nephites astray and caused them to sin by telling them there was no such thing as wrong-doing.

After preaching in Zarahemla, Korihor went to Jershon to try to persuade the people of Ammon. But they were wiser than many of the Nephites. They took Korihor, bound him, and carried him before Ammon, the high priest, who told them to take Korihor out of the land.

After leaving Jershon, Korihor traveled to Gideon to try to preach, but he did not have much success. The people bound him and carried him before the high priest and the chief judge of the land. They questioned him about his false teachings, and when they witnessed the hardness of his heart and how he even insulted God, they refused to speak to him. They bound him and sent him to Zarahemla before the chief judge Nephihah and the high priest Alma.

Jershon

Jershon is the Nephite land by the sea, south of the land Bountiful. The Nephites gave this land to the Lamanite converts, the people of Ammon, also known as the Anti-Nephi-Lehies. The Lamanites tried to murder the converts, but the Nephites protected them.

LAND NORTHWARD
Desolation
NORTH SEA
Narrow Neck of Land
NORTH SEA
BOUNTIFUL
Sidon River
Wilderness of Hermounts
ZARAHEMLA
Gideon
Ammonihah
Land of Jershon
Hill Manti
Hill Amnihu
Sidom
Minom
Aaron
East Wilderness
South Wilderness
Melek
Manti
Narrow Strip of Wilderness
NEPHI (Lehi-Nephi)
Helam
Middoni
Shilom
Midian
Mormon
WEST SEA
Jerusalem

Korihor spoke with big words and falsely accused Alma of depending upon the people for his living. Alma corrected him and said that he worked with his own hands, even though he traveled a lot and spent so much time serving the Church. After questioning him, Alma told Korihor that he was possessed of a lying spirit and that he had put off the Spirit of God. Korihor challenged Alma to show him a sign, or some physical proof, that God lived and that Alma spoke the truth. Alma replied that Korihor had been shown enough signs, since all things show there is a God. Korihor continued to reject the truth until Alma warned him that if he denied the truth again, Korihor would be struck dumb. And he was. Korihor could no longer speak.

Nephihah wrote Korihor a note, asking him if he was convinced of the power of God. Korihor wrote back that he knew it was the power of God that made it so he could not speak. He also wrote that he always knew there was a God, but that the devil had deceived him. Korihor said that the devil had appeared in the form of an angel and had told him many lies. After repeating those lies to the people, he believed they were true. Korihor asked Alma to remove the curse and allow him to speak, but Alma said, "It shall be unto thee even as the Lord will" (Alma 30:55).

Korihor spent the rest of his days going from house to house, begging for food. When he left the Nephites and went to the Zoramites, Korihor was "run upon and trodden down, even until he was dead" (Alma 30:59).

Gideon

Gideon is the Nephite land on the east of the River Sidon that was named after Gideon, the captain in the military during the reign of King Limhi who helped prevent war with the Lamanites. Righteous people lived in Gideon for many years, but much later, by the time Samuel the Lamanite preached, it was a wicked place.[20]

The Zoramites and the Rameumptom

A man named Zoram led his people east of Zarahemla to the land of Antionum so they could practice their own form of religion. Alma received word that Zoram and his followers, the Zoramites, bowed down to idols and had changed from the true way of worshipping God to their own way. They no longer kept the commandments.

When Alma heard about the Zoramites, he felt very sorrowful. But he knew that preaching the word of God would have a more powerful effect upon the Zoramites than fighting with the sword, so Alma organized a mission to the Zoramites. He took Ammon, Aaron, Omner, (the sons of Mosiah), Amulek, Zeezrom, and two of his three sons, Shiblon and Corianton.

Alma and the other missionaries were surprised when they arrived in Antionum and saw that the Zoramites had already built synagogues, where they gathered one day of the week. They worshipped

in a way that Alma and his brethren had never before seen. In the center of the synagogue, the Zoramites had built a platform that was high above the head, and only one person at a time could stand on the top of it to pray. Whoever wanted to worship would stand on the top of the tower, called the Rameumptom, stretch his hands toward heaven, and with a loud voice repeat the same prayer. The prayer included several false and evil ideas. It said that God was a spirit and always would be. It said that the Zoramites were God's chosen children, and that only they would be saved while everyone else went to hell. And it said that they did not believe in Christ. After the Zoramites repeated the deceitful prayer, they did not speak of God or pray the rest of the week.

Alma and the other missionaries were astonished and deeply saddened by what they saw and heard. They also noticed that the Zoramites set their hearts on gold, silver, and all kinds of precious things. They wore expensive clothes and jewelry and thought they were better than other people.

After praying for strength that they would be able to teach the Zoramites, Alma blessed the other missionaries, and they separated from one other. The missionaries tried to teach the Zoramites to believe in Jesus Christ, to have faith and repent, and to follow the teachings of the prophets in the scriptures.

Many of the Zoramites listened to the missionaries and were converted to the truth. They left to live with the people of Ammon in the land of Jershon. The remaining Zoramites became angry when they saw how many of their people were joining with the people of Ammon. The Zoramite leaders began to mix with the Lamanites on their borders and stir them up to anger. Together they made preparations for war, and the Nephites prepared to defend the people of Ammon and the Zoramite converts. Alma and the other missionaries returned to Zarahemla, grateful that they could help bring so many Zoramites to repentance but also sorrowful that the Lamanites were threatening war.

Shiblon

Shiblon was the second son of Alma the Younger. Like his older brother, Helaman, he remained a faithful missionary. Even when imprisoned and stoned by the Zoramites, he stayed true.

Corianton

Corianton was a younger son of Alma the Younger. He did not remain faithful on his mission. He committed serious sins. His father rebuked him. He sincerely repented and returned to the ministry.

Rameumptom

These Mesoamerican ruins show how the Rameumptom might have looked.

Faith Is Like a Seed

When Alma and the other missionaries were in Antionum among the Zoramites, they went into their synagogues, their houses, and even the streets to teach the people. With a lot of effort, the missionaries began to have success among the poor class of people. The more prosperous Zoramites had thrown the poor Zoramites out of the synagogues because they did not have fine clothes.

As Alma was speaking to a group of people on the hill Onidah, some of the poor Zoramites approached him. They asked him what they should do since they no longer had a place to worship. Even though they had helped to build the synagogues with their own hands, they were no longer welcome there because they did not have fancy clothes. Of course, Alma did not want the poor Zoramites to be treated badly, but he was joyful because he knew that their unfavorable circumstances had prepared them to hear the word of God.

Alma immediately quit trying to preach to the rich Zoramites, and he began speaking directly to the poor people. Alma praised them for being humble. He explained that while he knew many of them would be humble no matter what, it was better to be humble of their own free will than to be forced to be humble because of their poverty. He reminded them of the teachings of Zenos the prophet in the scriptures who said that people should pray and worship in all places. Alma told them that they should worship God all week long, not just once a week in the synagogue.

The poor Zoramites did not understand what it meant to have faith in God, especially in Jesus Christ who would come. Alma taught: "Faith is not to have a perfect knowledge of things; therefore if ye have faith ye hope for things which are not seen, which are true" (Alma 32:21). Alma helped them to

Synagogue

Like a church building, a synagogue was a place for people to worship and learn more about God. Today, synagogues are the centers of worship for people of the Jewish faith.

Zenos

Zenos was an ancient prophet whose writings were on the brass plates. The Nephites often referred to his teachings.

understand this idea by comparing faith to a seed. If faith is "planted" in a heart that is soft and open to the truth, it will grow and become knowledge. If the seed is not good, it will not grow; but if the seed is good, it will grow and enlarge the soul. He also explained how faith needs to be nourished, or cared for, so it will continue to grow and so its roots can dig deep into our hearts.

When Alma finished teaching, Amulek observed that the great question still in the minds of the poor Zoramites was about Jesus Christ. Amulek bore a powerful testimony to them that he knew Jesus Christ would come. He told them that Jesus would offer His own life as an atonement for the sins of all mankind. He encouraged them to plant the seed of faith in their hearts. He urged them to pray always and repent so they would be prepared to meet God.

Many of the Zoramites, especially those who were poor, listened and believed. Because they believed, the proud Zoramites threw them out of their land. The humble Zoramites joined with the people of Ammon in the land of Jershon.

Captain Moroni and Zerahemnah

Zoramites

Zoramites were once Nephites, but they rejected the truth and joined with the Lamanites. Once a week, they climbed a tower called the Rameumptom and recited the same prayer, never speaking of God again for the rest of the week. They loved their riches. The Zoramites thought they were better than other people. They no longer believed in Jesus Christ.

Breastplates, Armshields, and Shields

The Nephites wore arm-shields and breastplates and used shields to protect themselves during battle.

The proud Zoramites who did not listen to the missionaries eventually joined with the Lamanites. Thousands of Lamanites gathered in the land of Antionum (where the Zoramites lived) to prepare for war against the Nephites. Zerahemnah led them and stirred them up to fight. He wanted more power. His plan was to put the Nephites in bondage and rule over them. He assigned Zoramites and Amalekites to be their chief captains because they were more wicked and more willing to murder than were many of the Lamanites.

The Nephites saw that the Lamanites were getting ready for war, so they prepared to defend themselves. They gathered in the land of Jershon (where the Anti-Nephi-Lehies lived), and they made breastplates, arm-shields, shields to defend their heads, and thick clothing. Moroni was their leader. Though he was only twenty-five years old, he was brave, strong, and good. Moroni wanted to protect his people and preserve their freedom and privileges. He wanted them to be able to worship God.

The Lamanites had more than twice as many soldiers as the Nephites, but when the Lamanites approached Jershon and saw how well the Nephites had prepared themselves, they became afraid. They had only their weapons—almost no clothing and no shields. The Lamanites backed away into the wilderness.

As soon as the Lamanite armies retreated, Moroni sent spies to watch their camp. Moroni also sent men to the prophet Alma to ask him to ask the Lord where the armies should be sent. Alma prayed and received direction. The prophet told the messengers that the Lamanites were marching toward Manti to attack the weaker part of the Nephite people.

Moroni left part of his army in Jershon and took the rest of his army to Manti. He hid them on both sides of a river and also by a hill. When the Lamanites approached, the Nephites surrounded them and fought with great strength and courage. The Nephites were well protected, but the Lamanites fought so fiercely that, at one point, the Nephites almost ran away. Moroni reminded his armies why they were fighting: for their families, their lands, their liberty, and their freedom. The Nephites prayed aloud for strength and then encircled the Lamanites and triumphed.

Moroni ordered them to stop fighting. He spoke to the Lamanite leader, Zerahemnah, and explained that the Lord had delivered the Lamanites into their hands. Moroni commanded him to hand over their weapons and take an oath, or a promise, not to fight again. Zerahemnah handed Moroni his weapons, but he refused to make a promise for peace. Moroni gave the weapons back to Zerahemnah and told him they would not let them go unless they promised not to fight again. Zerahemnah became angry and raised his sword to kill Moroni. One of Moroni's soldiers hit the sword out of Zerahemnah's hand and took off Zerahemnah's scalp. Zerahemnah became angry, and the war started again.

After much fighting, Zerahemnah saw that they were about to be destroyed. He cried to Moroni and promised to take an oath if they would spare their lives. Moroni ordered the fighting to stop. The Lamanites made a covenant of peace, Moroni received their weapons, and the Lamanites returned to the wilderness.

Captain Moroni and the Title of Liberty

Rent Garments

Anciently, a rent gar-
ment, or a torn piece of
clothing, was an out-
ward sign of an inward
promise. The Nephites
promised to follow God
or else be torn from
His presence (like their
coats).

Taken up by the Spirit

Most scholars agree
that "taken up by the
Spirit" means that Alma
was translated, as were
Moses, Elijah, and oth-
ers. He went to heaven
without having to die.

In his old age, Alma blessed and counseled his son Helaman and put him in charge of the Church, and then Alma was taken up by the Spirit and never heard of again. Because of the wars with the Laman- ites and other disturbances among the Nephites, Helaman decided that the Nephites needed to hear the word of God again and that they needed to have rules and guidelines set up throughout the Church. Helaman and others traveled among the Nephites, teaching the gospel and establishing the Church.

Even though the Lord had spared their lives in battle and saved them from the Lamanites, some of the Nephites began to fall away from the Church. Helaman appointed priests and teachers to watch over them, but many began to disagree with him and would not listen. They were rich and proud of themselves and did not think they needed to listen to Helaman. They became angry and even wanted to kill the other Nephites. A large and strong man named Amalickiah flattered these rebellious Nephites and told them if they made him their king, he would make them rulers over the Nephites. Amalickiah was a skillful speaker and knew how to persuade the people to do wickedly. Many people followed him, and he stirred them up to want to destroy the Church of God.

Moroni was chief captain of the Nephites. When he heard about these rebellions, he tore off part of his coat and wrote on it: "In memory of our God, our religion, and freedom, and our peace, our wives, and our chil- dren" (Alma 46:12). He fastened it to the end of a pole and called it the title of liberty. He put on his headplate, his breastplate, his shields, and his armor. He took the pole with his coat on the end of it, and he bowed his head to pray. He prayed mightily for the blessings of liberty to rest upon his people as long as there were any true believers of Christ remaining.

When Moroni finished praying, he traveled among the people, wav- ing the title of liberty so all could read it. He called with a loud voice: "Whosoever will maintain this title upon the land, let them come forth in the strength of the Lord, and enter into a covenant that they will maintain their rights, and their religion, that the Lord God may bless them" (Alma 46:20).

The people came running with their armor and their torn coats, as a sign of the promise they were making to take upon them the name of Christ and not be ashamed. They threw their rent garments at Moroni's feet and promised to keep the commandments.

Amalickiah fled with his followers, but Moroni cut off their escape in the wilderness. Moroni told the Amalickiahites that they needed to covenant to support the cause of freedom or die. Almost all of them chose to covenant for freedom. Amalickiah and a small number of his men were able to avoid being caught by Moroni and the righteous Nephites, and they returned to the Lamanites.

The King-men and the Freemen

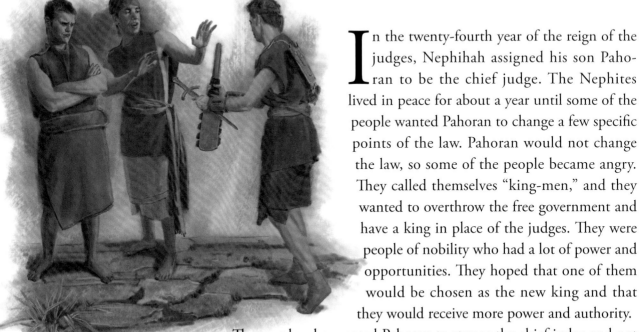

In the twenty-fourth year of the reign of the judges, Nephihah assigned his son Pahoran to be the chief judge. The Nephites lived in peace for about a year until some of the people wanted Pahoran to change a few specific points of the law. Pahoran would not change the law, so some of the people became angry. They called themselves "king-men," and they wanted to overthrow the free government and have a king in place of the judges. They were people of nobility who had a lot of power and opportunities. They hoped that one of them would be chosen as the new king and that they would receive more power and authority.

The people who wanted Pahoran to stay as the chief judge and not have a king replace him called themselves "freemen." They wanted to keep their rights and be able to worship God as they pleased. The Nephites decided to let the people choose which form of government they should use. Most people voted for the freemen rather than for the king-men.

At the same time, Amalickiah, the wicked Nephite who had run away from Moroni and had become the leader of the Lamanites, was gathering his armies. When the king-men heard that the Lamanites were coming to battle, they were glad in their hearts. They refused to pick up their weapons and help the Nephites defend themselves.

Moroni became angry when he heard that the king-men refused to fight. He had done so much to protect them, and he could not understand why they would not help defend their people, their land, and their liberty. He sent a petition representing the voice of the people to the governor. The petition asked the governor for permission to either force the king-men to fight or to put them to death. He knew that if the Nephites were divided, they would not be able to withstand the Lamanite attack.

Moroni commanded his army to attack the king-men. He wanted to humble them so they would be willing to defend their country. Moroni

Amalickiah

Amalickiah lied and murdered to become king of the Lamanites. He swore he would drink Moroni's blood, but he never did. Mormon wrote of Amalickiah: "We . . . see the great wickedness one very wicked man can cause to take place among the children of men" (Alma 46:9).

and his army lifted their weapons against the king-men and fought them to the death. They had to kill four thousand of the king-men and put their leaders in prison before the rest of the king-men agreed to help the Nephites. The conquered king-men agreed to raise the title of liberty on their towers and defend their country against the Lamanites. They no longer called themselves king-men.

In the meantime, Amalickiah had strengthened his forces and had begun attacking the Nephite cities. Weakened by the battles they had been fighting with their own people, the Nephites could not defend themselves against the Lamanites. Amalickiah and his forces took possession of many of the Nephite cities.

On their way to take over the city of Bountiful, the Lamanites ran into the Nephite captain Teancum and his men. Teancum and his men were great warriors—strong and skilled in warfare. They fought the Lamanites and gained advantage over them until it became too dark to fight. During the night, Teancum sneaked into the Lamanite camp, right into Amalickiah's tent. Teancum put a javelin into the king's heart. When the Lamanites awoke and discovered that their king had been killed, they feared the Nephites and retreated for a time.

Teancum

Teancum was a brave Nephite military leader who defeated Morianton's army and killed Morianton when they tried to take possession of the northern lands. Later, Teancum slew Amalickiah's brother Ammoron, but shortly thereafter he was killed by Ammoron's servants. Moroni said of him: "[he] fought valiantly for his country, yea, a true friend to liberty" (Alma 62:37).

Two Thousand Stripling Warriors

When the people of Ammon, or the Anti-Nephi-Lehies, listened to the missionaries and converted to Christ, they made an oath never to shed blood again. Even though they had been great warriors, they buried their weapons and promised not to use them. The Nephites welcomed the people of Ammon to the land of Jershon and agreed to protect them.

Many years passed, and the Lamanites took control of a number of the Nephite cities along the seashore. The people of Ammon saw how the Nephites gave their lives in battle and fought so courageously. They began to consider breaking their oath in order to help the Nephites defend themselves against the Lamanites.

Just when they were about to break their oath and take up weapons of war, Helaman convinced them that if they did, they might commit a great sin and lose their souls. Instead, their young sons, who had not made the oath, came forward and promised

Antipus

Antipus was a Nephite army officer appointed by Moroni to command some of the Nephite forces. His men were losing to the Lamanites until Helaman and the two thousand stripling warriors came to their rescue. Weak and tired from pursuing the Lamanites, Antipus lost his life in battle.

Stripling Warriors

We do not know the exact age of the stripling warriors when they went to battle, but scholars figure that they were probably between twenty and twenty-two years old. That would mean they were about seven years old at the time their fathers took the oath never to fight again.[21]

to join the Nephites in fighting for liberty. With Helaman as their leader, two thousand courageous young men volunteered to fight. Helaman called them his sons, and they thought of him as a father. They were righteous young men who were true at all times and who kept the commandments of God.

The stripling warriors went forth in the strength of the Lord. Their mothers taught them that if they did not doubt, God would deliver them. Their fathers sent many supplies to them and to the other Nephites. The stripling warriors led away the most powerful army of the Lamanites to the land northward. Then they turned back and fought courageously to help Antipus and his weary warriors gain victory over the Lamanites.

The next year, sixty more stripling warriors joined with their brothers as well as six thousand men from Zarahemla. They took the city of Cumeni. Just when the rest of the Nephite army was about to give in to the Lamanites, the 2,060 stripling warriors fought most desperately and drove the Lamanites back. After the Lamanites fled, Helaman surveyed his stripling warriors to see if any had been killed. All of them had been wounded and many had fainted because of the loss of blood, but not one of them had died. The rest of the army was astonished that none of the stripling warriors had been slain. They knew that it was a miracle and that God had preserved their lives because of their great faith. They trusted in God, and they were protected by His power.

Encircled by Fire

After years of peace, the Nephites began to forget how the Lord had blessed them. They loved their riches and did not help those who were poor. They boasted in their own strength and no longer kept the commandments. So when the Lamanites came to battle against them, the Nephites were weak and were driven out of their own lands.

Nephi became tired of the wickedness of the greater part of the people, so he gave up his judgment seat and decided to spend the rest of his life preaching the word of God. Along with his brother Lehi, Nephi reminded the people what the prophets had been teaching for many generations: believe in Jesus Christ, repent, and be baptized. Nephi and Lehi spoke with great power and had a lot of success in teaching the Nephites and even many of the Lamanites. Eight thousand Lamanites were baptized and joined the Church of God.

But when Nephi and Lehi left for the Lamanite land of Nephi to preach, a Lamanite army took them and put them in prison (the same prison where King Limhi had kept Ammon many years earlier). Nephi and Lehi did not have food to eat for many days. The guards even came to kill them, but when they saw Nephi and Lehi encircled by a fire that did not burn them, they did not dare touch them. Nephi and Lehi explained that it was the power of God protecting them, and when they spoke, the earth and the walls of the prison shook.

The prison guards and others who gathered became overshadowed with a cloud of darkness. The Lamanites heard a voice above the darkness telling them to repent and to stop trying to destroy His servants. Even though the voice spoke like a whisper, it was strong and pierced their souls. It shook the earth and the walls of the prison. The cloud of darkness remained, but the faces of Nephi and Lehi were filled with light as they looked toward heaven and spoke with angels. Fear overtook the Lamanites, and they asked Aminadab, one of the Nephite rebels who had joined them, what they should do. He told them to repent and pray until they had faith in Jesus Christ. They prayed with all their hearts, and as they did, the cloud of darkness went away. And they, too, were encircled by fire.

Nephi and Lehi were in the middle of the people, and they were all surrounded by a flaming fire, yet they were not burned. The fire did not spread to the prison walls; it only encircled the people. About three hundred people were there and felt unspeakable joy as the Holy Spirit entered their hearts. A pleasant voice from heaven spoke to them, as if in a whisper, and said: "Peace, peace be unto you, because of your faith in my Well Beloved" (Helaman 5:47). When they heard the voice, they looked toward heaven, and angels came down from heaven and blessed them.

The people left the prison and told those who were not there what had happened. Most of the Lamanites were convinced of the truth. They laid down their weapons of war, put aside their hatred toward the Nephites, and gave their hearts to God.

Moronihah

In the sixty-first year of the reign of the judges, Moronihah, who was a Nephite captain and also the son of Moroni, preached to the Nephites, along with Nephi and Lehi (the sons of Helaman). The Nephites began to repent. As they repented, they gained strength. Moronihah was able to lead them in recapturing half of their lands.

Nephi Prays for His People

Not many years passed before the Nephites fell into wickedness again. Evil men who belonged to the Gadianton robbers filled the judgment seats. They punished the good people for being righteous, and they let the wicked and guilty people go free.

Nephi felt so sad that his people were wicked that he poured out his heart to God in prayer. He prayed on top of his garden tower near a highway that led to the market. While he prayed, some people passed by and heard him. They ran and told others, so that when Nephi finished, he saw a crowd of people watching him pray. He talked with them and told them that if they did not repent, their lands would be taken from them and they would be destroyed.

When some of the wicked judges heard what Nephi had prophesied, they stirred up the people against Nephi. Some of the people joined with the judges, and some of the people defended Nephi. They knew he was a good man, and they did not think he committed a crime by telling them to repent. Nephi spoke to all of them about Jesus Christ. He

reminded them of the prophets who testified of Christ's coming and asked them how they could not believe after the evidences they had been given.

While he spoke to them, he received inspiration that would help show them God's power. Nephi told the people that the chief judge, Seezoram, had been murdered and that if they went to the judgment seat, they would find him lying in his blood. Five men ran to the judgment seat to see if it had really happened.

When the men approached the judgment seat, they found Seezoram dead, lying in his blood. They fell to the ground in astonishment and began to shake. They became afraid of Nephi's prophecy and what would happen to them if they did not repent. While they lay there, the people who were responding to the servants' cry of murder arrived. These people immediately thought the five men were the murderers, so they bound them and put them in prison.

The next day, the people gathered to bury the chief judge. The wicked judges were at the burial, and they asked what had happened to the five men. When they found out the men were in prison, they ordered that they be brought before them. The judges questioned the men and then released them. The judges decided that Nephi must have worked with another man to kill the judge. How else could he have known what happened? They said they would pay Nephi and not kill him if he would admit to murdering the chief judge.

Nephi spoke powerfully against their false accusation and gave them another sign. He told them that the chief judge's brother was the murderer and that they would find blood on his coat. Nephi told them to go to Seantum, the chief judge's brother, and ask him some questions. Nephi said Seantum would deny it at first, but if they pointed to the blood on his coat, he would confess to the murder. Everything happened exactly as Nephi said it would. The people saw how the power of God worked in Nephi, and many believed he was a prophet.

Gadianton Robbers

The Gadianton robbers were an evil band of robbers who tried continually to control the government and who entered into secret promises to hide their crimes. Gadianton was the name of one of their early leaders. "Gadianton did prove . . . almost the entire destruction of the people of Nephi" (Helaman 2:13).

A Famine in the Land

Sealing Power

The Lord told Nephi, "Whatsoever ye shall seal on earth shall be sealed in heaven; and whatsoever ye shall loose on earth shall be loosed in heaven" (Helaman 10:7). In our time, the sealing power was restored through Elijah the prophet in the Kirtland Temple. Whenever the fullness of the gospel has been on the earth, the Lord has blessed his people with the sealing power.[22]

Nephi was walking toward his house—thinking, praying, and feeling sad about the wickedness of the Nephites—when he heard the voice of the Lord. The Lord thanked Nephi for being so faithful in preaching the gospel, in keeping the commandments, and in doing His will. The Lord blessed Nephi with the sealing power, or the power to do anything God wanted him to do. The Lord knew Nephi would use this power righteously.

After receiving this great blessing, Nephi immediately turned around. Instead of going home, Nephi returned to the crowds of people and began preaching to them again. He repeated to them that they would be destroyed if they did not repent. But the people's hearts were hard, and they would not listen to him. They tried to put Nephi in prison, but he was protected by the Spirit of the Lord, and they could not lay their hands on him.

Nephi continued to preach to the people for many days; some listened to him and others did not. The people began to fight with each other. They even started to kill each other with their swords.

By the next year, wars raged throughout the land. Nephi prayed that they would not destroy each other by the sword. He asked God to bring a

famine to the land so the people would humble themselves, repent, and remember the Lord.

And so it was done. They stopped fighting with their swords because a great famine came to the land. Rain stopped falling, and crops would not grow. Thousands of people died because they had no food to eat. The famine continued into the next year, and the people began to wonder if they would all die. They pleaded with the judges to go to Nephi and ask him to pray for the famine to end.

When Nephi saw that the judges and the people had repented and humbled themselves, he asked the Lord to send rain and spare their lives.

The Lord heard Nephi's request, and rain began to fall. Both the Nephites and the Lamanites rejoiced! The rain made the crops grow, and once again, the people had food to eat. They no longer tried to destroy Nephi; they knew he was a prophet of God, and they were grateful that peace had been restored throughout the land.

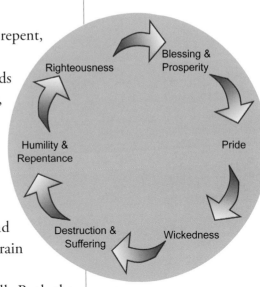

Blessing & Prosperity

Righteousness

Pride

Humility & Repentance

Destruction & Suffering

Wickedness

Pride Cycle

Throughout the Book of Mormon, when the people remembered God and kept the commandments, they were blessed. Not only were they happy, but they were blessed with food and shelter and other comforts. Sometimes, they became proud and forgot how the Lord had blessed them, and they stopped living righteously. Their lives would become difficult and, in their hardships, they would humble themselves and remember the Lord again. This process is sometimes called the pride cycle.

Samuel the Lamanite

By the eighty-sixth year of the reign of judges, most of the Nephites lived in great wickedness and were no longer keeping the commandments. Many of the Lamanites, however, were obeying the commandments and living righteously. Samuel, a Lamanite prophet, came to the Nephites in Zarahemla and preached to them for many days. The Nephites did not like what he said and forced him to leave the city.

Just when he was about to go back to his own land,

Samuel heard the voice of the Lord telling him to prophesy to the Nephites again. Samuel returned to Zarahemla, but they would not let him back into their city. So he stood on the wall of the city, stretched his hand out, and spoke with a loud voice. He spoke what the Lord put in his heart. Samuel told the Nephites that an angel had visited him, bringing glad tidings. Samuel wanted to share the good news with them, but they would not listen. He warned the people that they would be destroyed if they did not repent and have faith.

Samuel told them that Jesus Christ, the Savior of the world, would come in five more years. He gave them a sign of the Savior's birth: the night before His birth, there would be no darkness. Samuel explained that there would be a day and a night and a day as if it were one day and there were no night. He told them that a new star would rise and great lights would fill the heavens.

Samuel also gave the Nephites some signs of the Savior's death. Samuel explained that Jesus would live on the earth and then die so that they (and all people) might repent and live with Heavenly Father again. Jesus would offer His life to bring about the resurrection of all mankind. Samuel described the signs of Jesus' death: the sun, moon, and stars would be dark for three days. It would thunder and lightning for many hours. The earth would shake and tremble; mountains would be laid low and become valleys. Many highways would break up, and cities would be destroyed.

Some of the Nephites believed that Samuel spoke the truth. They searched for the prophet Nephi, confessed their sins, repented, and asked to be baptized. Others threw rocks at Samuel and shot arrows at him. Some of them saw that their weapons could not hit him, and they realized that the Lord protected Samuel. They, too, went to Nephi and asked to be baptized. But many others hardened their hearts against Samuel. They refused to believe him. Some tried to lay their hands on him, but he jumped down from the wall and ran away. The Nephites never saw Samuel the Lamanite again. He returned to his own land to preach and prophesy among his own people.

Resurrection

Resurrection is when a body that has died and its spirit come back together, never to be separated again. Because Jesus Christ broke the bands of death, all people will receive the gift of resurrection.

A Night without Darkness

Nephi, Son of Helaman

For almost forty years, Nephi served the people and prophesied of Jesus Christ. He lived at the same time as Samuel the Lamanite. Nephi baptized the people who were converted because of Samuel the Lamanite (see Helaman 16:3).

Nephi, the son of Helaman, gave the sacred records to his son Nephi and left Zarahemla. No one knows where the older Nephi went, but the younger Nephi kept the records and watched over the people. Some Nephites began to say that the time had passed for Samuel's prophecy of a night without darkness to be fulfilled. They caused a lot of contention, mocking those who believed and telling them that their faith in Jesus Christ had been for nothing.

The believers felt sad. They continued to watch for the night without darkness, but the unbelievers only mocked them more. The unbelievers became so wicked that they set a day when they would kill those who believed in Jesus Christ, unless the sign of His birth was given.

Nephi, the son of Nephi, felt sorrowful. He bowed down and cried mightily to God in behalf of his people. He prayed all day. Then he heard the voice of the Lord, saying: "Lift up your head and be of good cheer; for

behold, the time is at hand, and on this night shall the sign be given, and on the morrow come I into the world" (3 Nephi 1:13).

Just as the Lord had told Nephi, at the setting of the sun that day, there was no darkness. It stayed light for a day, a night, and a day. A new star appeared in the heavens, and everything happened as foretold. Those who had watched for the signs of Jesus' birth rejoiced. The unbelievers felt afraid and fell to the earth, as if they were dead.

Nephi and other righteous leaders went among the people teaching them, helping them to repent, and baptizing them. Most of the people believed and were converted to the Lord. Once again, the Nephites enjoyed peace in the land.

Years passed, and some of the people, especially the young people, began to lose faith. They began to be less astonished by the signs and wonders, and some even forgot them. Their hearts became hard, and Satan led many of them to believe that the doctrine of Christ was foolish. Many of the unbelievers joined the Gadianton robbers. They lived in the hills and stole from and murdered the righteous people.

The righteous Lamanites joined with the righteous Nephites and prepared to defend themselves against the Gadianton robbers. They left their lands and gathered their animals and food—enough to last for seven years. When the robbers attacked, they did not fear them. They looked to the Lord for strength, and they were able to defeat them. They thanked God for delivering them from their enemies.

Nephi, Grandson of Helaman

Nephi was such a righteous leader that angels ministered to him daily. When his brother was stoned and killed by the wicked people, Nephi raised him from the dead. Nephi performed many mighty miracles in the name of Jesus Christ.

The Coming of Jesus Christ

Hosanna

In Hebrew, *hosanna* means "save now, we pray thee." In Jerusalem, when Jesus entered the city during the last week of His life, the people waved palm branches and cried, "Hosanna!" Similarly, today, when we dedicate temples, we wave white handkerchiefs and say, "Hosanna, Hosanna, to God and the Lamb."

During the thirty-fourth year after the sign of Jesus' birth, people began to watch for the three days of darkness that Samuel prophesied. Many people doubted and argued with each other about the signs of Jesus' death.

One day, a terrible storm arose, unlike any they had experienced before. Thunder shook the earth. Lightning struck with such force that it lit the city of Zarahemla on fire. The city of Moroni sank into the sea, and a great mountain formed on top of the city of Moronihah. The tempests, whirlwinds, thunderings, lightnings, and earthquakes changed the appearance of the land. Many people died.

The storm lasted about three hours, and then a thick darkness fell. The mists were so dark that there was no light—not even from candles, torches, or fires. The sun, moon, and stars did not shine. People groaned in the darkness and cried out loud. Many people wished they had repented and listened to the prophets. The darkness lasted for three days.

In the darkness, the people heard the voice of Jesus Christ. The first time He spoke, Jesus told them to repent. He invited them to come unto Him so He could heal them and they could have eternal life. After they heard Jesus' voice, they were so astonished that they fell silent for many hours. They heard Jesus' voice again, reminding them how many times He would have gathered them as a hen gathers her chickens under her wings, but they would not. The people listened, and they began to cry again. They

felt so sad because many of their loved ones had died in the storm. On the morning of the third day, the darkness went away. The more righteous part of the people survived the storm.

A crowd of people gathered near the temple in the city of Bountiful. They were wondering together and showing one another the great changes that had taken place. While they were talking about Jesus Christ and the sign that had been given of His death, they heard a voice. They did not understand the voice. They looked around. The voice was not harsh or loud; it was a small voice, but it pierced their hearts so much that they shook. They heard the voice again, but they did not understand it. The third time they heard the voice, they looked toward heaven, and they understood. It was Heavenly Father's voice, and He said, "Behold my Beloved Son, in whom I am well pleased, in whom I have glorified my name—hear ye him" (3 Nephi 11:7).

They saw a man wearing a white robe coming down from heaven. He stood in the middle of them. They were completely silent. At first, they thought it was an angel. But He stretched His hand toward them and said, "Behold, I am Jesus Christ, whom the prophets testified shall come into the world" (3 Nephi 11:10).

The people fell to the earth. The Lord told them to rise, and He invited them to put their hands on His side and feel the prints of the nails in His hands and feet so they would know He was the God of the whole earth. One by one, they touched Him. They knew He was the Savior. They cried aloud, "Hosanna," and they fell at His feet and worshipped Him.

Jesus Christ Ministers to the People

After the people touched Jesus and saw the nail prints in His hands and feet, Jesus called the prophet Nephi forward. Nephi bowed down and kissed the Savior's feet. The Lord commanded him to arise, and He blessed Nephi. Jesus gave Nephi the power to baptize, and then Jesus called eleven others and gave them power to baptize. He taught them the correct way to baptize: they should go down into the water, speak the words of the baptismal prayer, and immerse the person in water. These twelve men became disciples of Jesus Christ; He called them to serve and minister to the people. Jesus told the people to listen to and follow the disciples.

Jesus taught the people the gospel. He delivered a sermon similar to one He gave on the Mount of Olives in Jerusalem. It included the Beatitudes—a series of teachings that describe a spiritual quality and the blessing that goes with it. For example, Jesus taught: "Blessed are all the pure in heart, for they shall see God" (3 Nephi 12:8). He told the people to let the light of the gospel shine from inside of them to others.

The people had been living the law of Moses, and Jesus explained that it was fulfilled in Him. He said that the law was given to help them believe in Him, repent of their sins, and come unto Him with a broken heart and a contrite spirit.

Jesus showed the people how to pray. He commanded them to forgive each other, to fast, and to seek for heavenly treasures, not earthly rewards. Jesus promised the twelve disciples that if they would seek first the kingdom of God and His righteousness, they would find the food, clothing, and shelter they needed. Jesus taught the people not to judge one another. He encouraged them to ask God for direction and help, and He warned them not to listen to false prophets.

Law of Moses

The law of Moses was a system of commandments and rituals that God's people followed from the time of Moses until Jesus Christ. The Israelites practiced this lesser portion of the law to prepare themselves to receive the fulness of the gospel of Jesus Christ. The sacrifices taught the people mercy and forgiveness. Just as people could offer a pure animal as a sacrifice on their behalf, we can seek forgiveness and peace because Jesus Christ, the sinless Son of God, offered His perfect life.[23]

Before Jesus' resurrection, He told the people in Jerusalem that He had other sheep, or followers of the true gospel, who were not of that fold. Jesus explained to the people in Bountiful by the temple that they were the "other sheep," and then He told them that He had other sheep than they. He assured them that He would go to them also, and that there would be "one fold and one shepherd" (3 Nephi 16:3).

Jesus noticed that the people seemed weak. They had been listening to Him for a long time, so He told them to go home, ponder on what He had said, and prepare to be taught by Him again the next day. But the people were in tears; they looked as if they wanted Him to stay with them a little longer. So He invited them to bring their sick and afflicted forward. One by one, He healed them. They all bowed down, even those who were well, and they worshipped Him. Many came forward and kissed His feet and bathed His feet with their tears.

Jesus Christ Blesses the Children and Administers the Sacrament

Same Day

From the time Jesus first appeared to the people gathered by the temple until He ascended to heaven was the same day. (3 Nephi 11:1 to 3 Nephi 19:2 happened in one day.)

After Jesus taught the people and healed the sick, He commanded the people to bring their little children to Him. They brought their children and set them on the ground around Jesus. When all the children were gathered near Him, Jesus stood in the middle of them and commanded the multitude to kneel. Jesus also knelt down and began to pray to Heavenly Father. Joy filled their souls as they listened to Him pray for them.

When Jesus finished praying, He arose, but the people did not. Jesus told them to rise, and He blessed them because they had such great faith. He told them His joy was full, and then He wept. He took the children, one by one, and blessed them and prayed unto the Father for them. And then He wept again.

The people looked up and saw the heavens open. Angels descended out of heaven, as if they were in the midst of fire. They came down and encircled the little ones, and they, too, were encircled by fire. The angels ministered to the children, and the people watched. About two thousand and five hundred souls witnessed this marvelous event.

Later, Jesus told His disciples to bring some bread and wine to Him. When the disciples returned, He took the bread and broke and blessed it.

He commanded the disciples to eat it, and when they had eaten, He told the disciples to give it to the multitude. Jesus said that He would give them authority to bless and break the bread and that they should administer it as He had shown them. He explained that the bread would remind them of His body, and when they partook of it, it would be a testimony to the Father that they remembered Jesus. And by remembering Jesus, they would be blessed to always have His spirit with them. Next, Jesus blessed the wine and told His disciples to drink and then give it to the people. He explained that the wine would remind them of His blood that He shed for them, and it would witness to the Father that they remembered Him. And if they always remembered Him, they would have His spirit to be with them.

He commanded them to meet together often, to partake of the sacrament, and to watch and pray always. Jesus taught the people to welcome others to church, not to cast them out, but to pray for them and be good examples to them. He urged the people to be at peace with one another and not to argue.

Jesus told them that He must go to the Father for their sakes. He laid His hands on His disciples, one by one, and gave them power to give the Holy Ghost. After laying His hands on each of the disciples, a cloud overshadowed the people so they could no longer see Jesus. But the disciples watched Him ascend into heaven.

Bread and Wine

The bread used by Christ for the sacrament was most likely unleavened bread. The wine was more like grape juice and did not make the people drunk. When Jesus reappeared the next day, He miraculously supplied the bread and wine for the sacrament.

Jesus Christ Establishes His Church

After Jesus ascended to heaven, the people returned to their homes and spread word of His appearance. All night long, the people made great efforts to gather to the place where Jesus had been. The next morning, Nephi and the other disciples stood before the crowd, but since so many people had gathered, they separated into twelve groups. The twelve disciples taught the people and prayed with them. They prayed for what they most desired: that the Holy Ghost would be given to them. The Twelve went down to the water to be baptized. Nephi was baptized, and then he baptized the disciples Jesus had chosen. After they were all baptized, they received the Holy Ghost. The crowd of people saw that the Twelve were encircled about as if by fire. Angels came down from heaven and ministered unto them.

While the angels attended the twelve disciples, Jesus came and stood in the middle of them. Jesus directed the people to kneel down and pray. As they prayed, Jesus went a little way off and bowed down to pray. He thanked Heavenly Father for giving the Holy Ghost to them. Jesus smiled when He saw the disciples still praying, and His countenance shone upon them.

Jesus directed the crowd to stop praying but to always

The Three Nephites

Before Jesus returned to Heavenly Father, He asked His disciples what they desired. Nine of the disciples wanted to return speedily to live with Jesus. But three of the Nephites requested that they might never die so they could stay and help people. Jesus blessed them according to their desires, and those three were changed. They would live forever as disciples of Jesus Christ. Even when wicked people threw them in prison, buried them in pits, cast them into fiery furnaces and dens of wild beasts, they were never harmed. Three hundred years later, they ministered to Mormon and Moroni.

keep a prayer in their hearts. He taught them His gospel. Jesus reminded the people that all the prophets had testified of His coming. He explained that they were the children of the prophets, or the covenant people through whom all the people of the earth would be blessed. He reviewed scriptures with them and spoke to them of His Second Coming.

Jesus taught them the importance of keeping records. He asked Nephi to bring their records to Him. Jesus read what had been written and asked why they had not recorded all that Samuel the Lamanite had prophesied and how it had been fulfilled. He commanded them to write the things they had heard and seen. Jesus also commanded them to write the words of Malachi. He talked to them of a book of remembrance, and He told them that the world would be judged out of the books which have been written.

For three days, Jesus taught the people, and after that, He appeared to them often. Jesus taught and blessed the children. When the children were with Jesus, they spoke marvelous things. Even the babies could talk, and they spoke such marvelous things that the people were commanded not to write them down. The disciples began to baptize the people, and they were filled with the Holy Ghost. When the disciples asked Jesus what they should call the church, Jesus answered: "Ye shall call the church in my name" (3 Nephi 27:7). And so the Church of Jesus Christ was established among the Nephites.

The Prophet Mormon

For many years after Jesus Christ came to the Nephites, they lived in peace and unity. They were not divided into Nephites and Lamanites or any kind of "ites." The people shared all that they had with one another, so they were neither rich nor poor. They kept the commandments, and the disciples of Jesus performed many miracles: they healed the sick, they raised the dead, and they blessed the blind to see and the deaf to hear. The people prospered in the land and rebuilt Zarahemla and other cities that had been burned.

After about two hundred years of living righteously, a small part of the people rejected the Church and called themselves Lamanites. Some people in the Church began to be prideful, thinking they were better than other people because they had fancy clothes and expensive things. They no longer shared what they had with one another. They began to form other churches that recognized Christ but rejected important parts of His gospel. One of the churches even denied Christ and persecuted the true Church. Many of the people hardened their hearts and willfully rebelled against the gospel of Jesus Christ, even teaching their children not to believe.

After three hundred and twenty years had passed away since the appearance of Jesus Christ, the Nephite record keeper Ammaron hid the sacred records in a hill because the people were so wicked. He then spoke with a boy named Mormon who was only ten years old. Mormon was a serious and clear-minded child who was quick to observe what was happening. Ammaron asked Mormon if he would keep the records for their people when he grew older. He told Mormon that he had hidden the plates in the hill Shim, and he instructed Mormon to get the plates when he was about twenty-four years old.

So much wickedness had spread throughout the land that the Lord took the three Nephite disciples away, and the work of miracles and healings stopped. The Holy Ghost did not come upon any of the people because they had become so wicked and no longer believed.

The Lord visited Mormon when he was fifteen years old. Mormon felt and knew of the goodness of Jesus. He wanted to preach to the people and tell them to repent, but the Lord told him not to because the people's hearts were so hard. Gadianton robbers infested the land; sorceries, witchcraft, magic, and evil power prevailed.

In his sixteenth year, Mormon became the leader of the Nephite armies. He was large in stature and brave of heart. When the Lamanites attacked, the Nephite armies retreated at first. The Lamanites drove them out of their cities. Mormon tried to unite the Nephites and inspire them to repent, but they continued to falter. Even though Mormon's armies were always outnumbered by the Lamanites, Mormon encouraged them to fight for their wives, their children, and their homes. After years of fighting, Mormon and his men finally withstood the Lamanites and forced them to leave the Nephite land. The Nephites and Lamanites then made a treaty and divided the land.

The Record Keepers

The prophet Nephi gave the records to his son Amos, and Amos gave the records to his son Amos. Before Amos the younger died, he gave the records to his brother Ammaron who entrusted them to Mormon.

The Final Battles

The Nephites made a treaty with the Lamanites, and they enjoyed peace in the land for ten years. During this time, Mormon may have retrieved the plates from the hill Shim, studied the scriptures, and prepared the sacred record, the Book of Mormon, that would bring people to Jesus Christ and prepare them for His Second Coming.

After ten years of peace, the king of the Lamanites sent a letter to Mormon warning the Nephites that they were preparing for war. Mormon gathered his people to the city Desolation by the narrow pass. The Nephites strengthened themselves, so when the Lamanites attacked, they drove them back to the land southward. The next year, the Nephites fought off the Lamanites again.

The Nephites started to brag about how well they could fight. They did not remember the Lord, and they did not repent of their sins. Even though the Lord delivered them from their enemies three different times, they did not acknowledge Him. They only hardened their hearts against the Lord.

They had become so wicked that Mormon refused to lead his people when they decided to attack the Lamanites. The Lamanites drove the Nephite armies back to the land Desolation. The Nephites were still tired from fighting when the Lamanites attacked again and took over the city. The next year, the Lamanites attacked the Nephites who fled to the city Teancum, but this time the Nephites fought them off. Again, the Nephites bragged about their skills in battle and took back the city Desolation.

The Nephites and the Lamanites fought for many years, but the

The Book of Mormon

Mormon put together a sacred record of his people from the plates he received. The Plates of Nephi consisted of the (1) large plates, a historical record that Mormon shortened into the Plates of Mormon, and (2) the small plates, a spiritual record. Mormon also included many of the prophets' writing from the brass plates, the ancient record Nephi brought from Jerusalem that contained their history and the writings of the prophets. Mormon's son Moroni added the Plates of Ether to the record.

Nephites never gained power over the Lamanites again. The Lamanites began to sweep the Nephites off the land. Mormon could not bear to see his people suffer. Even though they remained wicked, Mormon decided to lead them again. The Nephites had a few small victories, but they could not fight off so many Lamanites.

Almost ten years later, Mormon, as an old man, wrote a letter to the king of the Lamanites asking if he could gather the Nephites by a hill called Cumorah for what would become the final battle. Mormon hid the records in the hill Cumorah, except for a few that he gave to his son Moroni. The Lamanites attacked and killed over two hundred and thirty thousand Nephites. Mormon was wounded, and only twenty-four Nephites (including his son Moroni) survived the battles. Some Nephites ran away, and some joined the Lamanites. Mormon cried for his people: "O ye fair ones, how could ye have departed from the ways of the Lord! . . . How could ye have rejected that Jesus, who stood with open arms to receive you! Behold, if ye had not done this, ye would not have fallen" (Mormon 6:17–18).

The Brother of Jared and the Jaredites

The Book of Ether

King Limhi (see Mosiah 8:9–10) gave Ammon twenty-four gold plates that some of his people had found among the ruins of a great nation. Ammon brought those records to King Mosiah, who translated them (see Mosiah 28:17) and told the people about the history of the Jaredites. These gold plates, called the Book of Ether, were added to the rest of the records that were passed down. Moroni wrote a shortened version of the records and added them to the record his father Mormon had prepared.

The Jaredites were a group of people who left the old world more than a thousand years before Lehi left Jerusalem. At the time of the tower of Babel when the Lord confused the languages, Jared asked his brother to pray for mercy. He prayed that their family and friends would still be able to understand each other. The Lord had compassion on them and did not change their language. The Lord told them to gather their families, their flocks, and seeds of every kind and prepare to live in a land of promise. They carried fish in a vessel they built, and they also took birds with them. They even brought swarms of bees so they could have honey in the promised land.

The Jaredites traveled to the valley of Nimrod. While they were there, the Lord came to them. He was in a cloud, so they could not see Him, but they heard His voice, and He directed them. They traveled in the wilderness and then built barges to cross the many waters. The Lord continually directed them until they came to the great sea that divided the lands, and they pitched their tents along the seashore.

Four years later, the Lord came to the brother of Jared again and stood in a cloud and talked with him for three hours. The Lord scolded the brother of Jared for not calling upon Him. The brother of Jared repented, and the Lord told him to prepare to leave for the promised land. The Lord told the brother of Jared to build barges, similar to the ones they had already built.

The brother of Jared and the Jaredites built eight barges. Each was the length of a tree and tight like a dish so water

could not get into it. The Lord told them to make a hole in the top and in the bottom of each barge so they not only could unstop the hole to get air, but also so they could plug the hole when big waves crashed upon them. The brother of Jared did as the Lord commanded.

But how would they get light into the vessels? The Lord asked the brother of Jared what he would have Him do so they could have light. Windows would be dashed to pieces, and they could not take fire into the tight, wooden boats. The brother of Jared went to Mount Shelem and melted out of a rock sixteen small stones that were white and clear. He carried them to the top of the mount and asked the Lord if He would touch them with His finger so they might shine in darkness. The Lord touched the stones, one by one, and they began to glow with light.

The brother of Jared saw the Lord's finger touch the stones and then he saw Jesus Christ's whole person. The brother of Jared had such great faith that the veil was taken from his eyes. The Lord told the brother of Jared that as He appeared to him in the spirit, He would one day come into the world and appear in the flesh.

The Brother of Jared

The brother of Jared was the Jaredite prophet who led his people to the promised land. His name is not given in the Book of Mormon, but the Prophet Joseph Smith revealed that his name is Mahonri Moriancumer.[24] He had a perfect knowledge of God.

The Jaredites and the Prophet Ether

After the Lord touched the stones the brother of Jared put before Him, the Jaredites set one stone in each end of their boats and left for the promised land. The stones shone in the darkness of their covered boats and gave them light. A strong wind drove the Jaredite boats on the water for almost a year, 344 days, until they landed at the promised land.

As soon as the Jaredites arrived, they bowed down and thanked the Lord. They shed tears of joy and gratitude for His tender mercies toward them. They began to till the earth and plant their seeds. They had children, and their children had children, so that by the time Jared and his brother were old and about to die, there were many, many Jaredites inhabiting the land.

Jared and his brother asked the people what they would like before they died, and the people said they wanted a king. The brother of Jared did not like the idea, and he prophesied that a king would lead them into captivity, but Jared encouraged his brother to choose a king. So they chose the oldest son of the brother of Jared. Neither that son nor any of his brothers agreed to be the king. None of the sons of Jared agreed to be the king either—except for one named Orihah. Orihah was a righteous king, and so was his son, Kib, after him. But many years later, Kib's son Corihor rebelled against his father and drew away many of the people.

Corihor was the first of many wicked rulers among the Jaredites. He gathered an army and put his father and his father's people in bondage,

already fulfilling the prophecy that a king would lead their people into captivity. Over the course of hundreds of years, the kingdom passed from one king to another. Some of the kings were righteous, and while they ruled the people, the Jaredites prospered and were blessed. But many of the kings were wicked. They formed secret combinations to gain power, and they led the people to worship idols. Prophets came to the wicked Jaredites and told them to repent, but most of the people rejected the prophets.

Ether was the last prophet who lived among the Jaredites. He preached from morning until evening, telling the people to believe in God and repent. He taught them about faith, hope, and charity. He explained that the Lord gives us weaknesses so we might humble ourselves and draw near to Him. Ether told the Jaredites to seek Jesus. Eventually, the Jaredites cast him out of their city. He hid in a cave during the daytime, and at night, he observed what was happening to his people. While he stayed in the cave, he finished the record of his people. After witnessing their entire destruction, he hid the records, and hundreds of years later, the Nephites found them.

Coriantumr and Shiz

Coriantumr was the last Jaredite king and the only survivor of the Jaredite wars. He first rejected Ether and tried to kill him, but later he repented when he saw Ether's prophecies being fulfilled. He tried to end the fighting with his enemy, Shiz, but the Jaredites no longer had the Spirit of the Lord with them and they were so "drunken with anger" (Ether 15:22) that they would not stop fighting. Thousands of people, including women and children, died in the battles. Coriantumr was wounded many times. In the final battle, only Shiz and Coriantumr were left to fight. When Shiz fainted from loss of blood, Coriantumr cut off his head.

The Prophet Moroni

Mormon's son, Moroni, was the last writer of the Book of Mormon. His father, all of his family, and his friends had been slain in battle. He was alone, and he had no safe place to stay. The Lamanites had become so wicked that they killed any Nephite who believed in Jesus Christ. Moroni had seen the Lord and talked with Him face to face (see Ether 12:39). He would not deny Jesus Christ, so he hid from the Lamanites to save his own life and to protect the sacred records his father had entrusted to him.

While in hiding, Moroni wrote a shorter account of the Jaredites, or the Book of Ether. Moroni had seen the coming forth of the Book of

Mormon. He said that the Lord had shown us, the people of the latter days, to him and that he knew the difficulties we would face. He warned us not to be prideful. Moroni reminded us to care for the poor, the hungry, the sick, and the afflicted.

Moroni also wrote to the Lamanites of future generations. Even though Lamanites threatened to kill him, Moroni knew that someday their children's children would want to know the truth. He desired to help them, and all honest seekers, to find and recognize the truths of the gospel of Jesus Christ. He wrote about repentance, baptism, and the gift of the Holy Ghost. Moroni explained the purpose of the sacrament and the correct way to administer it. He included the sacrament prayers for the bread and for the water.

Two different times Moroni thought he was finished writing because he was sure the Lamanites would capture and kill him. But he decided to keep writing as long as he could. Moroni included some of the teachings of his father. Mormon had spoken in the synagogue about faith, hope, and charity. Moroni wrote his father's words: "Charity is the pure love of Christ, and it endureth forever" (Moroni 7:47). Moroni also included a letter his father had written about little children, how good and innocent they are. Some people thought babies and very small children needed to be baptized, but Mormon had asked God and learned the truth: "Little children need no repentance, neither baptism. . . . Little children are alive in Christ" (Moroni 8:11–12).

Moroni sealed the sacred book with his testimony of Jesus Christ for all future generations and finished by inviting all people everywhere to come unto Christ.

Moroni's Promise

Moroni promised everyone who really wants to know if the Book of Mormon is true that if they ask God in prayer, He would let them know it is true by the power of the Holy Ghost (Moroni 10:4).

The Gold Plates

The Gold Plates

The plates were about six inches wide, eight inches long, and six inches deep. Three silver rings held the plates together. The plates were most likely not made of pure gold because gold would be too soft for writing and extremely heavy. They were probably a combination of gold and copper, and they weighed about fifty pounds! The engravings on the plates were in reformed Egyptian because its characters took less space than Hebrew writing.[25] When Joseph finished translating the gold plates, he returned them to the angel Moroni.

In the spring of 1820, while praying fervently about which church to join, Joseph Smith received the First Vision, in which God the Father and His Son, Jesus Christ, appeared to him. They told him not to join any of the churches that were then in existence.

Three years later, on September 21, 1823, seventeen-year-old Joseph Smith was kneeling in prayer when his bedroom filled with light. A heavenly messenger, the angel Moroni, told Joseph about the gold plates. The angel left and came back two more times that night and once in the morning. Each time he told Joseph the exact same thing: sacred scriptures, engraved on gold plates, were hidden under a large stone on a hill near Joseph's home.

The next day, Joseph climbed the hill and scraped the dirt away from the big rock. He found a lever and, with all his strength, used the lever to lift the rock until he could see a stone box. He looked in the box and saw the gold plates! He reached for them, but a familiar voice stopped him. The angel Moroni told Joseph he could not take the plates yet; the angel told Joseph to meet him at that same place in one year.

The next fall, Joseph climbed the Hill Cumorah, removed the big rock, and saw the gold plates. Again, the angel Moroni met Joseph and taught him. He let Joseph hold the gold plates, but he told him not to set them down or put them out of his hands for a moment. The plates were precious because the word of God was written on them.

The next September and the next, Joseph climbed the Hill Cumorah, dug up the big rock and saw the gold plates. Joseph listened carefully when the angel Moroni told him about the prophets who lived a long time ago. Their stories and teachings of Jesus Christ were written on the plates. Joseph knew that he had been called by God to bring them to the world.

Finally, four years after he first saw the gold plates, twenty-one-year-old Joseph and his new bride, Emma, left during the middle of the night to bring the gold plates home. Emma waited with the horse and wagon at the bottom of the hill while Joseph went to that familiar rock. Emma watched and waited, alone in the dark, for half the night and into the morning. At last, Joseph came down the hill carrying something very heavy in his big, loose shirt. Joseph had been given the gold plates!

OLIVER COWDERY

DAVID WHITMER

MARTIN HARRIS

The Witnesses

At least thirteen people saw the gold plates: Joseph Smith; the Three Witnesses, Oliver Cowdery, David Whitmer, and Martin Harris, who also heard the voice of God and saw an angel; and the Eight Witnesses (listed in the front of the Book of Mormon), as well as Peter Whitmer Sr.'s wife, Mary.

108

The Translation and Publication of the Book of Mormon

Urim and Thummim

The Lord gave Joseph Smith the Urim and Thummim—two clear stones that were fastened to a breastplate—to help translate the gold plates.

From the day Joseph Smith brought the gold plates home, wicked people tried to steal them. At first, Joseph hid them in the hollow of an old birch tree near his home. But when he thought they were no longer safe there, he wrapped them in his shirt and looked for another hiding place. As he was walking through a thicket, he heard footsteps behind him. A man leaped from the bushes, hit Joseph with his gun, and demanded that he give him the gold plates. Joseph fought the man off, and then fought off two other men. He ran a couple of miles home that day—all the while holding the heavy plates close to his heart.

Joseph locked the gold plates into a wooden chest. He hid the chest under the stones of the family's fireplace. When a mob of angry men came to steal them, Joseph and the other men in the family ran out the doors toward the mob and yelled as if they were commanding an army. The mob became scared and ran away. But the angry men did not give up. They kept trying to hurt Joseph and steal the plates. Finally, Joseph and Emma buried the gold plates in a barrel of beans, put the barrel in the back of a wagon, and left Palmyra.

Joseph and Emma found peace for a while with Emma's parents in Pennsylvania. In time, they moved to a small farmhouse nearby where Joseph could translate the writing on the gold plates. By the gift and power of God, Joseph looked through the Urim and Thummim and could read the unfamiliar writing. Joseph's friend Oliver Cowdery sat near him and listened carefully; he

Grandin Printing Press

The printer E. B. Grandin ran his printing press fourteen hours a day, six days a week, for seven months in order to print the first copies of the Book of Mormon.

wrote down the English words that the prophet read. Before spring turned to summer, Joseph had translated most of what was written on the gold plates. But just when Joseph was about to finish, some townspeople started to threaten him again. Joseph, Emma, and Oliver quickly left for New York.

Meanwhile, the Lord prepared the Whitmer family in Fayette, New York, to receive a prophet of the Lord. When Joseph came to them, they welcomed him warmly. During his stay with the Whitmers, the Prophet finished translating what was written on the plates. The light of heaven filled their home. In that blessed but humble home, The Church of Jesus Christ of Latter-day Saints would later be organized, but not before the gold plates became the Book of Mormon.

Joseph found a printer in Palmyra, New York, close to his family home, who agreed to typeset the handwritten pages. Joseph's friend Martin Harris sold most of his farm to pay the three thousand dollars needed to print five thousand books. Joseph's family and close friends helped keep the record safe while it was being printed. In the spring of 1830, ten years after Joseph Smith first saw Heavenly Father and Jesus Christ, the Book of Mormon was published.

Family Home Evening Suggestions

At least a year's worth of family home evening lessons can be found in this book. Each chapter is a self-contained lesson. The sidebars offer important supplementary information, the illustrations help younger children engage in the stories, and the stories themselves can be read aloud or retold.

Families with younger children might enjoy reading a story together and then acting out what they read. Children could prepare simple costumes and take turns acting in various parts. "Tents" could be made of sheets. Strips of fabric could be the sea or the wilderness. Stair banisters could be the iron rod, and so forth. The scriptures will come to life as children first become familiar with a story and then act it out.

Families with slightly older children might like to connect the scripture story with the teachings of our modern prophets. A quick search on lds.org can connect the scripture story with talks that prophets have given or with articles published in Church magazines. As older children prepare to teach a family home evening lesson, they can first read the retelling of the scripture story in this book and then make connections with gospel truths.

Parents might use the stories as springboards for discussing gospel topics. The format of this book allows for a quick review of the stories, and the stories lend themselves to discussion and teaching. King Benjamin's counsel to parents resounds through the ages: " . . . ye will teach [your children] to walk in the ways of truth and soberness; ye will teach them to love one another, and to serve one another" (Mosiah 4:15).

Notes

1. *Book of Mormon Student Manual,* 5.
2. Largey, *Book of Mormon Reference Companion,* 643.
3. Largey, 748.
4. Nibley, 128–29.
5. Largey, 445.
6. Valletta, *Book of Mormon for LDS Families,* 6.
7. Chadwick, 118.
8. Packer, 52.
9. *Book of Mormon Student Manual,* 47.
10. Largey, 784.
11. Smith, *Teachings,* 300.
12. Smith, *Gospel Questions,* 3:203.
13. Largey, 169.
14. Largey, 474–75.
15. Largey, 609.
16. Largey, 61.
17. McConkie, 340.
18. Largey, 593.
19. Largey, 67.
20. Largey, 293.
21. Tvedtnes, 28.
22. McConkie, 683.
23. Largey, 504–5.
24. Reynolds, 282.
25. De Groote, "Golden Plates."

Resources

Book of Mormon Student Manual: Religion 121–122. Salt Lake City: The Church of Jesus Christ of Latter-day Saints, 1989.

Chadwick, Jeffrey. "Lehi's House in Jerusalem and the Land of His Inheritance." In John Welsh, David Seely, and Jo Anne Seeley, *Glimpses of Lehi's Jerusalem.* American Fork, UT: Covenant Communications, 2004.

De Groote, Michael. "The Golden Plates: Just How Gold Were They?" *Deseret News,* 8 July 2010.

Largey, Dennis L. ed. *Book of Mormon Reference Companion.* Salt Lake City: Deseret Book, 2003.

McConkie, Bruce R. *Mormon Doctrine.* Salt Lake City: Bookcraft, 1966.

Nibley, Hugh. *An Approach to the Book of Mormon.* 3d ed. Salt Lake City: Deseret Book and Provo: F.A.R.M.S., 1988.

Packer, Boyd K. "Candle of the Lord." *Ensign,* January 1983, 51–56.

Reynolds, George. "The Jaredites." *Juvenile Instructor,* 1 May 1892, 282–85.

Smith, Joseph Fielding. *Answers to Gospel Questions.* 3 vols. Salt Lake City: Deseret Book, 1975.

Smith, Joseph Fielding, comp. *Teachings of the Prophet Joseph Smith.* Salt Lake City: Deseret Book, 1976.

Tvedtnes, John A. "I Have a Question." *Ensign,* September 1992, 28.

Valletta, Thomas R., ed. *The Book of Mormon for Latter-day Saint Families.* Salt Lake City: Bookcraft, 1999.

Acknowledgments

After almost two years of immersing myself in the Book of Mormon, I feel to acknowledge the divine power by which that book came forth. Nothing less than the hand of God could have lifted that book into the hands of a humble young man, Joseph Smith, and then guided its translation in roughly three months' time. After working to retell these scripture stories, my fervent testimony is that the Book of Mormon is the word of God.

I feel to acknowledge the scholars of ancient scripture who helped me bring historical accuracy and interest to this book. While their contributions are annotated at the back of the book, I especially want to thank the editor and contributors of *Book of Mormon Reference Companion* and *The Book of Mormon for Latter-day Saint Families.* They were invaluable resources.

I gratefully acknowledge the talented people in Deseret Book's publishing department. First and foremost, I want to thank Jana Erickson who guided this book through to completion. I am indebted to my editor, Leslie Stitt, for her editorial sharpness and sensitivity and to Tonya Facemyer for her precise, professional typesetting. And I am so thankful to graphic designer Shauna Gibby who directed the visual elements of this book.

I am awe-inspired by Brian Call's illustrations; he truly brought the stories to life.

Finally, I want to thank my husband and children for their love and support. Such a spiritually sensitive project simply could not have been undertaken without the steady flow of support that I had from them.

—Karmel Newell

I am grateful to a loving Heavenly Father who has helped me accomplish this wonderful project. Special thanks to my wife, Michelle, and my family for sacrificing their time with me while I painted. Also, many thanks to my family, ward members, and students for being such great models and for helping me bring the Book of Mormon stories to life.

—Brian Call

Additional Illustration Credits

Art Resource, 21

Bassitart/Shutterstock, 104

Steve Bunderson, 23

Tom Child, 45, 64

Gustave Doré/public domain, 20

Shauna Gibby, 82, 109

Jerry Harston, 85

Intellectual Reserve, Inc., 97, 106, 107

Lester Lee, 31

Stephen Orsillo/Shutterstock, 5

Steven Reed, 108

Julius Schnorr von Carolsfeld/Wikimedia, 9

Shutterstock, 27, 40, 50, 59, 63, 67, 72

Rui Valede Sousa/Shutterstock, 57

Thinkstock, 2, 3, 7, 8, 10, 13, 14, 15, 19, 25, 26, 29, 31, 32, 36, 39, 43, 47, 53, 54, 69, 70, 88, 91, 92, 93

Thinkstock/Jupiter Images, 17

Unknown source, 24

Lucas van Valckenborch/Wikimedia/public domain, 34

Edwin M. Wolley, 48

Index

About the Author

Karmel Newell holds bachelor's and master's degrees in English literature. She has served on a general Church writing committee, as a Relief Society president, and as a Primary president. She has written other books for children and loves being with children—her own and others. Reading the Book of Mormon together with her husband, Lloyd, and their four children is one of her abiding joys.

About the Illustrator

Brian Call graduated from Brigham Young University with a bachelor's degree in fine arts. Since that time, he has worked as an illustrator, creating artwork that has appeared in numerous magazines, books, and educational materials. He currently teaches in the art department at Brigham Young University–Idaho in Rexburg, Idaho. Brian and his wife, Michelle, and their six children live in Ammon, Idaho.